Fare Stage Series
Vol

BEDFORD BUSES
OF THE
1950s AND 1960s

Mike Berry

Trans-Pennine Publishing

CONTENTS

Front Cover: *Representing Bedfords in both the 1950s and 1960s, is this scene at Ulsta Pier on the Shetland island of Yell. On the left is VAS-Bella Vista BJX 848C, and on the right SB-Duple Vega KWX 412, both of which are now preserved and discussed in the text.* **Gordon Jamieson**

Rear Cover Top: *One of the stylish Duple Vega 'butterfly-grilled' SBs registered NDM 250.* **R.W. Berry**

Rear Cover Bottom: *The new order, a Bedford VAM70 with a Duple Viceroy C45F body.*

Title Page: *A batch of six Bedford SBs with MkII Vega bodies ordered by Rickards wait to leave the Duple works at Hendon, the coaches carry two liveries and are registered OLU 526-528 and OGT 308-310.*

This Page: *With a registration plate just right for the National Union of Railwaymen (NUR 17), this 'Big Bedford' had a Duple Vega C33F body. This stylish coach was actually operated by Simmons of Letchworth.*

Opposite Page: *Bringing back a few personal memories, this Bedford SB (MCX 386) was Fleet No. 348 in the Hanson fleet in my home town of Huddersfield. With its Plaxton Consort body, it is seen at an 'open day' at the town's ICI Leeds Road plant in the summer of 1961.*

The **Nostalgia Road** Series ™
is conceived, designed and published
by
Trans-Pennine Publishing Ltd.
PO Box 10
Appleby-in-Westmorland
Cumbria, CA16 6FA
Tel. 017683 51053
Fax. 017683 53558
ISDN. 017683 53684
e-mail trans.pennine@virgin.net
(A Quality Guild registered company)

Reprographics
Barnabus Design & Repro
Threemilestone, Truro
Cornwall, TR4 9AN
01872 241185

And Printed in Cumbria by
Kent Valley Colour Printers Ltd.
Shap Road Industrial Estate
Kendal, Cumbria LA9 6NZ
01539 741344

This Book Is Dedicated To
BOB BLUNDELL
With Thanks For All His Kindness

© Trans-Pennine Publishing & Author 2001
Photographs: Vauxhall Motors or as credited

INTRODUCTION

Having been involved in bus preservation for some years, firstly with the East Pennine Group and now with the Mersey & Calder Bus Preservation Group (both at Huddersfield), I was delighted to be asked to write a book on buses for the **Nostalgia Road** series. In addition to my current involvement with the preservation scene, my involvement with buses goes back more years than I care to admit. As a young boy, I recall my father coming home from work, often covered in wood-shavings, from his work as a coachbuilder. Just before World War II he had obtained an apprenticeship with the famous bodybuilders, Charles H. Roe Ltd. of Leeds. A wartime injury plagued his career in the years that followed, but when he was able to work, he remained in the business throughout the 1950s and 1960s.

During the early 1960s, my brother and I would occasionally get a treat on a Saturday morning and be taken into the workshops of Hanson's in Huddersfield, where the firm's large fleet of vans and coaches were repaired. The Hanson service buses would be used whenever we went to visit my grandparents at Lindley, in rattling Roe-bodied AEC's that we affectionately called the Hanson Tanks.

Later, as an apprentice mechanic, I would travel to work on the Huddersfield Corporation Leyland PD3s, which were then my favourite buses. A few years back I bought an ex-Leeds City Transport AEC Regent V/MCW Orion double decker of 1960 vintage, and became a diehard Southall supporter. So I was a bit bemused to find this book was to be about Bedford! Vauxhall cars maybe; after all one of my favourite models was the VX 490, but Bedford buses? Thoughts of the all-too common OB and OWB came to mind, for when compared to the throaty power of my 9.6 AEC, these models seemed like Dinky toys.

But, when I became involved in the restoration of an early (and unique) SB coach, I began to realise that Bedford had quite a lot going for them. In fact, at one time Bedford accounted for over 50% of all British single deck bus and coach chassis, and the Marque made a significant contribution to the industry. Coupled with the very kind support we have received from Vauxhall Motors, who have made available the official records and also a superb selection of photographs, this project was one I just had to undertake. I hope, that after reading it, you too will become a convert to the fascinating Bedford range of buses.

Michael P Berry,   Huddersfield, May 2001

THE BIG BEDFORD - THE STORY OF THE SB

This is really an account of how a marine engineering company became one of the world leaders in bus and coach chassis production, and it may sound strange to begin with a reference to boats, but as we pointed out in our companion book, *Vauxhall Cars 1945-1964*, the maritime industry was where Vauxhall Motors began their existence. Founded by Alexander Wilson, a Scottish engineer, the Vauxhall Iron Works was situated in Wandsworth Road, on the south bank of the River Thames. Here they produced marine engines and pumps for the growing maritime industry.

Wilson had left the company by 1894, and financial difficulties loomed. In 1896 J H Chambers was appointed as the Official Receiver, but rather than liquidate the business, he saw that it had great potential. So he restructured the business and from 1897 it became the Vauxhall Ironworks Company Ltd. Later that year Chambers, and F W Hodges (the Chief Engineer) built a petrol engine for a launch called the *Jabberwock*, and this engine later became the basis for the first Vauxhall car in 1903. Around 43 5hp single-cylinder 989cc automobiles were built in the cramped workshops alongside the ongoing marine engine. Despite good reviews, it was evident that a more powerful engine was needed and the 1904 model developed 1093cc. This car was entered in the London to Glasgow reliability trials, where it did surprisingly well.

Recognising that their cars would sell well, the company moved production to a new 7-acre site at Luton in Bedfordshire, because of the lack of space in the London factory. From these small beginnings the works eventually grew to occupy a 300-acre site. The history of Vauxhall's car production, is already covered in other **Nostalgia Road** books, but we must consider a few stages of the development, due to its association with the development of Bedford commercials. Most significant was the year 1907, when a split was made with the marine engineering business and Vauxhall Motors Ltd. was formed.

Although the development of the Vauxhall range was primarily centred on automobiles, a few were fitted with commercial bodies. The main development into this field came during World War I, when a large number of Vauxhall car chassis were bodied as ambulances and military vehicles. Following the war, Europe was plunged into a deep financial recession, and it dramatically affected the British motor industry, not least of all Vauxhall Motors.

In 1925 A P Sloan Jnr. paid $2.5 million for Vauxhall and it thereafter became part of the American General Motors organisation, who were already building trucks and buses in Britain. In 1931 the firm expanded into commercial vehicles, and the story of how they developed their range of Bedford PSV chassis is already told in our companion book, *Bedford Buses of the 1930s & '40s*.

Top Left: '*You take the high road.....*' *this particular high road being the main road from Ullapool to Lochinver, which is still 'unmade' in this 1952 view of Scottish Motor Traction's FFS 887. This SMT-bodied Bedford OB was typical of many Scottish bus operations in the 1950s and 1960s, but the OB lasted well into the 1970s and (in some cases) the 1980s in more rural parts of Britain.*

Top Right: *When the OB chassis was discontinued, many operators rebelled and Bedford were forced to continue production of an O Type bus, and it used the OL lorry chassis for the purpose. This famous example owned by Lewis of Greenwich carried the unique Duple Sportsman body on the OLAZ chassis.*

Middle Right: *The advent of the Big Bedford SB in 1950-1, with its 33-seat capacity was a major step forward and the SB range would have considerable longevity. But for many the most attractive buses on this chassis were the 'butterfly-grilled' Duple Vegas. This example, PMJ 222 was the Bedford demonstrator, but note that it carries the name Vauxhall Motors and not Bedford. At this time Bedford products sold like 'hot cakes', and publicity was needed for the firm's range of cars more than it was for the commercial vehicles!*

Bottom Right: *Sent to Coventry! In 1965 a batch of Marshall-bodied Bedford VAS service buses were acquired for the city's circular rail bus service. Operating on a 10 minute (peak) 20 minute (off-peak) frequency, fleet no. 507 (CRW 507C) carried passengers at four-pence a time.*

The start of Bedford's success was really their intuitive grasp of how the market would perform in the 1930s, and what the customer was looking for. General Motors already had quite a firm share of the British commercial vehicle market with their Chevrolet brand. This had become very popular in Britain after World War I, but there was a real need to have a 'British' product. Thus was born the British-built Chevrolet, which overcame some of the objections - but not all. Furthermore, following the Wall Street Crash in October 1929, there emerged something of an anti-American sentiment within British industry, as it was being said that Britain's economic problems could be laid fairly and squarely at the doors of the financial institutions in the USA. To overcome this, it was felt that the Chevrolet brand should be dropped in Britain, and something more prosaic adopted.

The answer was to follow a policy adopted by the Hudson Car Company who had problems marketing their British-assembled models before World War I. To overcome this, the chose they name of Essex for their range of cars, as their British assembly plant was based in that county. As stated later, if you look at material released by Vauxhall, it will frankly reveal that they do not know why the name Bedford was chosen for their range of commercials. Yet a search of contemporary records in the USA reveals that it was nothing other than a marketing ploy, and one that was based very firmly on the physical location of the manufacturing base.

Above: *Today 'football coaches' are usually very expensive commodities and often short-lived, especially if the team does not perform well. Of course back in the 1950s we would have called 'football coaches' team managers, and a football team coach would have been something like this SB-Duple Vega operated by Charlton Athletic Football Club. Seen here in the spring of 1952 is MLF 41, which is fitted with extra fog lamps and glass roof quarter lights. This picture was taken when the team were in Division One of the Football League (now the Premier League), as the SB was waiting to leave the Valley stadium for an away match. Perhaps it was the game on 19th April, when Charlton Athletic lost one-nil to Huddersfield Town! Like both Charlton and Huddersfield the coach soon faded from front line glory and finally ended up as a groundsman's shed at the club.*

Left: *The heart of it all, the SB (petrol) engine, which later became known as both the SBG and the 300. Simple, inexpensive and reliably robust, it was the start of a new era in motor coach operation.*

Top Right: *In August 1950 Vauxhall sent three prototype SB chassis to the body-builders, Duple in Hendon. These were SBD1, SBD3 and SBD4, as they were to be bodied for display at the Commercial Motor Show that October. The identity of these coaches has never been fully detailed, but one of them (SBD3) still remains today. I have spent many a happy hour underneath the old girl in the garage of my friend Gordon Jamieson of Cullivoe, Shetland. Re-registered in August 1951 as KWX 412 after its life as a demonstrator in the West Riding of Yorkshire, it went to Kildare of Ardwick, then to Heaps of Leeds, Leasks of Lerwick, Johnson of Scalloway, Hugh Sinclair of Yell and was finally bought by Gordon for preservation.*

Bottom Right: *A view of the SB chassis SBD1 taken in July 1950. Notice the low-height of the chassis, which has been achieved by 'dropping' it over the rear axle. The crown of the rear axle arch was, however, prone to collecting dirt and eventually would rust badly.*

As the pictures on the following pages show, Bedford's main bus chassis for the 1950s was the SB, but the SB's success did not just happen. To set the scene we need to look back at the earlier bus models! Whilst some may wonder why we are going back over ground covered in our earlier book, I feel it is essential to set the scene for the success that the SB gained in the 1950s. This success can be firmly traced to another policy that Vauxhall introduced in the depressed years of the 1930s, namely the production of a good range of highly dependable, but truly economic truck and bus chassis. Make them cheap and sell them quick was a philosophy that gained instant success, but simplicity of design also helped the range become truly dependable.

In the early days the Bedford WHB and WLB series buses were the first stage into the assault on traditional bus chassis manufacturers like AEC, Albion, Dennis, Karrier, Leyland, Maudslay, Thornycroft and the like. All of these firms, with perhaps the exception of Dennis and Karrier, had adopted a big bus policy, and it was obvious to Vauxhall that there was room for something in the smaller-lighter end of the market. By using a chassis in the 2- to 3-ton range, they would be able to offer an 'economy' chassis to the new type of bus operators who were beginning to open up the roads in the country and inter-urban districts.

Naturally AEC, Leyland and so on had already established themselves in the large fleet and municipality operators, where bigger buses were needed to move large numbers of people wishing to travel. In the rural districts it was a different story, as few bus services operated in these districts, and railway links were not always convenient. Hence, as the countryside began to demand public transport, operators had to take a gamble on whether a service could be economically justified. The viability of the service often depended on the economies of operation, and hence a lightweight, cheap to run, inexpensive bus chassis would undoubtedly be a major consideration. In fact not only did Bedford address this need, but it also went some considerable way in developing dual purpose goods-passenger carrying chassis such as the VYC and VXC 'Rural Bus' for country districts. All of this is covered in Alan Earnshaw's earlier book, but it is important to cover the basics.

7

Top Left: *Surrounded by United Automobile service buses at Newcastle's Elswick Street bus station, we see a Duple Vega on an early SB chassis. Number 12 in the Moor Dale fleet, OVK 505 was considerably more luxurious than the Bristol PSVs alongside it, as passengers on the route to Danby would probably testify.*

Centre Left: *Although the Duple Vega was more luxurious than those ECW service bodies, it was still quite utilitarian. It had Dean seat frames fitted with rather slim squabs and backs covered in short-pile cut moquette. More comfortable seating was available, but such ostentatious luxury was frowned upon in the postwar years. Yet, by 1952, extra luxuries were becoming more acceptable, and the result was the Duple Elizabethan. Here we see OKJ 210, owned by Raymond Way of Kilburn, being photographed in Luton for the commercial trade magazines of the day.*

Bottom Left: *The Duple Elizabethan was designed to show the world how British industry had recovered after the war, and this was done by providing free trips to and around London during the Coronation. The high class interior of the coach is shown in this view, which clearly reveals the on-board WC, galley and hostess service.*

The next stage was of course the WTL and WTB, which was developed from the WT 3-ton truck introduced at the 1933 Commercial Motor Show. This chassis, usually bodied by Duple, became the mainstay of light coach operation in Britain for the rest of the 1930s, and was only just being phased out in favour of the OB when war broke out in September 1939. The OB (and its war-time variant the OWB) could both fill books in their own right, but suffice it to say they were the basis on which many of today's modern coach companies were founded. Furthermore, the Government considered the OB to be such an economical vehicle, that it chose this as the only single-deck chassis type it would allow to be produced during the war years!

Following on from the success of the 1930s and 1940s, demand for Bedford and Vauxhall models, had grown to such a degree by the end of the decade, that the Luton factory had built almost 39,000 Bedford's, and 45,000 Vauxhall cars within 1949 alone. It was therefore decided that more production space was needed. To this end, a £10 million (£180,000,000 at today's prices) expansion project was launched, which was to include a new production building built on a 19½-acre site.

By 1950, Bedford had started production of a completely new bus/coach chassis from this factory. In March 1950, a new engine was unveiled for the popular OB chassis, which in hindsight may seem strange - but it was just another stage in the overall development. The new unit named the 'Extra Duty' engine was in the same form as its predecessor, being a petrol engine of six-cylinders and 28hp, although being upgraded to produce 84bhp. This was a vast improvement on the 1939 engine, which produced 72 bhp. New features in this unit included copper-lead main and big-end bearings, a Zenith carburettor, and re-designed induction and exhaust manifolds. The new engine was to prove not only more powerful, but more economical as well.

Alas, by the end of the same year the decision was made that the famed OB chassis had run it's course, after sales of 16,000 chassis, which included over 3,000 of the wartime OWB bus chassis. Vehicle designations by Bedford in the early years were very basic and uncomplicated. As mentioned previously, the OB was the O chassis in bus/coach form, so too the OWB was the same chassis but built in the war years, and was usually bodied to a very bland and basic design (usually with wood slatted seating). Even though some were re-bodied after the war they kept their W designations. Obviously to define this, Bedford merely inserted the W in the chassis designation for this purpose. One variant of the OB coach as depicted in the *Bedford Transport Magazine* around the same time as the new engine, was first shown at the 1950 Brussels Show. Having bodywork built by Van Hool of Belgium, it had a rather ungainly wide appearance, but amazingly was stated to have seating for 36-passengers! A substantial number of OBs are still in preservation to this day, and indeed some are still running commercially, albeit on 'specialised' heritage services.

One of Bedford's boldest moves to date appeared at the 1950 Commercial Motor Show, at that time held in London. Unveiled in October of that year was the new 7-ton commercial vehicle chassis, designated the S range, which included an all-new passenger chassis, the SB. This was to be Bedford's first foray into the full forward control chassis market for civilian use. Prior to this development, the only full forward control Bedford vehicles were the QL military models, although some of these were fitted with bus bodies for export with many going to Cyprus. Due to the high ground clearance of these chassis, they were ideal for traversing rough country terrain, and a few found themselves in the home market for specific duties. The main user being Southport Corporation who employed them on the long sandy beaches of that Lancashire seaside resort. Another Bedford forward control attempt prior to the new chassis, was built around the OB. One such coachbuilder to achieve this in Britain was the Willenhall Coachwork company. Some foreign companies tried this adaptation on their own vehicles, seeing it as a way to extend the life of their buses.

Top Right: *This stylish and highly unusual body fitted to the SB was built by the Arlington Motor Company, who were major Vauxhall-Bedford dealers. It had 33 'luxury seats' and featured some distinctive finishing touches. Note the enclosed rear wheel arches, revised radiator grill, deep side windows and large front screen.*

Centre Right: *When Duple were unable to complete its orders for the Vega body due to industrial action at Hendon, the firm turned to Brush at Loughborough to build bodies under licence. The first one of these, CNH 402 for Robinsons Coaches, is seen here after completion in July 1951.*

Bottom Right: *Another 'minor' builder on the SB was Gurney-Nutting, and their distinctive styling is seen on NPW 473. Pictured here in Kings Lynn, it was one of nine Bedfords then in the two-tone green and white livery of Carter's of Marham.*

The SB was not only a completely new innovation from the Bedford stable, it was also - at 324¼ inches (8.24 metres) - their longest chassis to date. But even though the new chassis was some 32 inches (81cm) longer than the previous OB design, the early SB buses were still only bodied to cater for 33 passengers. Considering that the earlier OB was capable of carrying 29-seat bodywork in luxury form, and the service bus body on the Utility OWB could accommodate 32 passengers, the full potential of the new length was not really realised.

As had become the norm with Bedford, the primary body builder was Duple Motors & Bodies of Hendon, who allowed the Scottish Motor Traction (SMT) company to build bodies to their design under a licence arrangement. This followed a practice that had been adopted with the Duple bodies on the W and O series, but Duple were not the only coach-builders who found the SB a profitable chassis to build on. As the pictures in this chapter show, several firms would eventually go on to body the SB, and Bedford did not try and restrict bodywork to a single manufacturer. The other main builders in the early years being Plaxton, Yeates and Burlingham.

However the first brochure, produced for the 1950 Commercial Motor Show, showed only models bodied by Duple. These were:- The Duple Vega 33-seat Luxury Coach Chassis on the Big Bedford Passenger Chassis at £2,320 (or £38,140 in today's money). The other option was The Duple Mk VI 33-seat Service Bus on the Big Bedford Passenger Chassis at £2,055 (£37,894). The price of the chassis was listed at £770 (£14,198). Four chassis were built in readiness for the show, these being SBD1, SBD3, SBD4 and SBD5. We believe that SBD2 was a left-hand drive chassis that was sent to the Vauxhall plant in Belgium.

Of the show models, SB4 was given the full specification, with X-type luxury seats, roof quarter lights, seven toughened glass roof panels, radio and de-mister. It was later registered JTM 129, and appeared on the main stand in a blue and cream livery. SB3 was painted red and cream and had the service bus specification but it also had luggage racks (it later become JTM 131 and then KWX 412). Finally, SB1 was painted in two tone green and had the basic Duple Vega coach specifications, we think it carried the works trade plates JTM 127, for a short while at least.

10

Top Left: *A pair of second generation SBs in service with Orange Coaches in May 1954; on the left a Harrington-bodied example (OXO 116) is seen awaiting to depart London with the Ramsgate/Margate express, whilst the Duple Super Vega on the right (OLL 460) is on the Brighton/Worthing express run. The London-based Orange Coaches had a long association with Bedford and Duple, and one of their Directors Keith Davies designed the KD coach body with Duple.*

Top Right: *When the improved Duple Vega SB combination was launched at the 1953 Commercial Motor Show, some substantial orders were placed. One such was this order for 12 SBs, which were delivered to Wessex Coaches by Duple in the spring of 1954. Registered SAE 951 to SAE 962, the new vehicles make an impressive line-up.*

Centre Right: *Another delivery that year was this Duple Vega (545 BMK), which was supplied to the British Overseas Airways Corporation (BOAC) in August 1954. Like many airport buses, the rear seats were replaced by a full-height luggage compartment (and large rear doors). This was one of a batch of SBs purchased for use at London (Heathrow) airport, where the new coach is seen in front of a BOAC Strato-cruiser named* Canopus.

Bottom Right: *Another SB Duple Super Vega (TTN 174) is seen here at Newcastle in 1956 with Moor-Dale Bus Services Limited.*

At this stage it is probably useful to give the full specifications for that first SB chassis, and in this respect we are fortunate to have the original 1950 Commercial Motor Show brochure that was produced by Vauxhall for reference. Quoting from that we read:

'The new Big Bedford passenger chassis is an outstanding example of modern engineering design and modern production techniques. Its 206-inch wheelbase provides ample scope for really roomy 33-seater luxury coachwork, and its many advance design features will appeal strongly to all operators. An outstanding feature is the comfortable ride ensured by carefully balanced weight distribution and springing with hydraulic shock absorbers and low-pressure tyres.

The big six-cylinder petrol engine develops 110 brake horse power. This large reserve of power permits the use of a high axle ratio, so that when cruising at 30mph in top gear the engine is turning over at only 1,635rpm. In addition to long engine life and fuel economy, these slow revving qualities ensure exceptional smoothness and silence. A synchromesh gearbox, with silent helical second and third gears, and hypoid bevel drive to the axle are other features which make for silent operation.

Duple Motor Bodies Ltd. have designed for the Big Bedford a 33-seater Luxury Coach and a 33-seater Service Bus bodies. These bodies are styled to match the modern chassis design and have been planned for manufacture on volume production lines with the advantages of low price and readily available replacement body panels and other components. Yet individual choice is assured in colours, upholstery and styling.'

Above: *Undoubtedly, one of the most attractive Duple designs ever to emerge from Hendon, was the 'butterfly grill' Vega. Fitted on the SB chassis, it became one of the most popular coaches of the mid-1950s. They were purchased by operators large and small, in my home town of Huddersfield no less than six firms employed two or more of these body-chassis combinations. This example, TLJ 201, is pictured in 1957, whilst taking excursion passengers from the seaside resort of Bournemouth to the Isle of Wight ferry at Lymington Pier. This service, operated by Shamrock & Rambler was very popular and several journeys a day were run during the holiday season.*

Left: *In order to demonstrate the popularity of the Duple Vega we show this interior shot of an 'oval grill' model taken at the Duple works in March 1954. The picture illustrates the 35-seater luxury version, with roof lights and roof quarter lights and tubular luggage racks. This coach was used on a regular service from London to France, Belgium and Switzerland.*

Top Right: *This superbly turned out Duple Vega was new to the Shetland operator John Leask & Son in May 1956. Registered PS 2627 it was the first vehicle that was driven regularly by the current MD of Leasks, Peter Leask. After service with several operators it was sold for use as a garden shed. At the time of writing, this 7 foot 6 inch (1.98m) wide coach still survives in a derelict state. J. Leask & Sons*

Centre Right: *A distinctive feature of the Duple Vega, was its 'speed styling' formed from chrome trim on the sides. However, not all models were given this embellishment, as confirmed by this model built for the United States Navy (91-01452).*

Bottom Right: *The firm of David MacBrayne Limited pioneered the steamship link between the Highlands and the Western Isle, before adding motor coaches and trucks to the fleet. At the time of this picture in September 1958, they were one of the most important transport units in the Highlands. Besides 20 steamers and 11 ferries they had 107 buses and 25 trucks with Bedfords strongly represented.*

The frame of the new SB was a cold squeezed rivetted construction, with six cross-members joining the 10-inch (25.4cm) deep main frames. The frame was arched over the rear axle, then dropped at the rear of this to provide space for an extra large luggage locker. Engine accessibility was a special feature of the design, and access was gained either from the cowl to the side of the driver, from the front (behind the radiator) or below. The front end tin-work was attached by 'quick-release' fasteners, which allowed the engine to be withdrawn for major overhaul in the minimum amount of time.

The engine itself was significant, and yet of such a simple design that it was a delight to work on. It was a petrol engine of 300.7 cubic inch capacity and gave 110bhp at 3,200rpm. Maximum torque was 234lb/ft and was developed at the low revs of 1,200 rpm. It was mounted on three widely-spaced rubber insulated brackets, had slip-fit cylinder liners of centrifugally cast-alloy iron, and a seven-bearing crankshaft. Compared to what had gone before, it was superbly balanced, and this helped the quiet, smooth running ride. Drive was delivered through a four-speed gearbox, which had synchromesh on 2nd, 3rd and top, through a three-piece prop shaft to a new hypoid rear axle.The drive line employed four Hardy-Spicer needle-roller-bearing universal joints, and two intermediate double-row sealed roller bearings.

Brakes were hydraulically operated with vacuum-servo assistance at the front, whilst these in turn operated mechanical rods which actuated the rear brakes. The master cylinder operated the two systems as one, while effectively isolating one from the other in case one system failed to operate. The vacuum servo unit took a bit of knowledge to master it, but in a very short time drivers of the SB found that servo assistance was proportionate to the pressure applied on the pedal. This made it very easy to spread the braking. Importantly, the system also provided direct connection between the pedal and the master cylinder when the engine was not running. The actual braking on all wheels was by two drum brakes per wheel, operated by bisector expander.

The early SB brochures were superseded in March 1953 with a 12-page colour catalogue (B516/3/51), and this document gives us full details about the Duple bodies. Obviously both the Vega coach, and the Mark VI service bus were built to fully comply with current Ministry of Transport regulations. The basic body shell was the same on both types of body, a full-fronted, forward-control offering embellished with polished moulding reliefs. They were of double truss-framed construction with rolled and folded steel framing and stressed interior panels. However, composite (timber and metal) framing was also available, subject to availability of good quality hardwood, which was then in very short supply nationally.

The roof was a full swept-dome type, with the front panels made from 16swg aluminium. A sliding panel sunshine roof came as standard, but seven toughened glass roof panels could be specified as an optional extra at £35.0s.0d (£455).

Body panelling was 18swg aluminium (except on the swept roof domes), and these panels were easily replaceable as they played no part in the coach's overall body strength. A sliding door was provided on the nearside, and an emergency door on the offside just behind the driver. A full width-bulkhead, half-height was fitted behind the driver's seat and between the two doors. There were variations to this arrangement though, and the photograph archive shows partial width bulkheads that give crew access in various places, and even full height bulkheads that enclosed the driver. Generally there were no seats next to the driver, but some coaches (eg: the Duple Elizabethan) carried a single courier seat in this position. The driver's seat was normally positioned above the battery box, but an optional extra on 'service bus' specifications was for a re-positioned battery box (on the opposite side of the engine cowl) and a swivelling driver's seat to allow one man operation.

Top Left: *The next major body development for the Bedford SB by Duple in 1959 was the attractively-styled Super Vega. This was to be the coach for the early-1960s. As a medium-sized coach, the body worked equally well as 'Yeoman' on the Thames Trader chassis. I particularly liked this design of body, and its features are seen to good effect on Bedford-Duple demonstrator (YNM 10) in 1960. Note the 'printer's cap' sun-visor at the front; this could be ordered with orange, green, blue, or clear Perspex panels.*

Top Right: *A later SB Duple Super Vega demonstrator is seen here with a three-piece windscreen. It features a completely different grill, altered side trim, sliding window vents and a one-piece front roof panel. It went to the Northern dealers Adams & Gibbon in 1960.*

Centre Right: *Here we see either an SB1 or SB3 Super Vega (713 CTM), at Old Warden before entering service with Alpine Prince.*

Bottom Right: *In 1962 Cunard Eagle Airways put into service three Bedford SB-Duple Super Vega coaches to transport passengers from their London terminal to Heathrow. One of the coaches (7941 ML) was used to carry press representatives from the terminal to the airport on Monday 30th April to attend a reception that marked the arrival of the first Boeing 707 ordered by Cunard Eagle. The picture shows the coach and the £2.2 million (£216,000,000) aircraft at London airport. The Bedfords were actually operated by Charles W Banfield, of Peckham on behalf of Cunard Eagle.*

Passengers were provided with considerable comfort, but the heater placed centrally on the front bulkhead did not endear itself to rear seat passengers in winter. Seats were sponge-rubber (rubberised-horsehair on the service bus) and finished in moquette on the coach or plastic hide on the service bus. The synthetic covering on the service bus tended to crack after a short period of time, and although moquette could be obtained as an extra at £61.0s.0d (£1,003) many operators took the cheaper option and lived to regret it. As a consequence, many MkIV Vega Service Bus bodies were fitted with other forms of seating or re-upholstered within a few years. One such was KWX 412, which was fitted with a set of Plaxton coach seats whilst it was in the ownership of Heaps of Leeds in or around 1953.

As a consequence of the internal refurbishment of the MkIV, it is often difficult to tell if an early Duple Vega started out in life as a coach or a bus. The easy way to tell a service bus would be the absence of boot and luggage racks, but as both of these features were available as optional extras, at £35.0s.0d (£575) and £40.0s.0d (£658), this is no guarantee. The MkIV may have been cheaper, and £265 (£4,208) was a significant sum of money in 1951, but Duple realised that it was very much a false economy. Indeed, so many customers came back to have their service buses uprated to full coach, that the service bus option was dropped when the improved model was launched in 1953. Extras on the coach included a 31-seat luxury seat variant and tubular parcel racks with interior lighting in place of the standard rack.

Top Left: *Although listed in Vauxhall records as being a Mulliner-bodied SBO, XDH 297 actually had a Willowbrook B39F body. It was part of a small fleet supplied to Walsall Corporation Transport (XDH 294-299) in July 1956. Carrying fleet numbers comparable to their registration numbers (ie: 294-299) number 297 is seen under the trolley bus wires outside the Birchills Bus Depot. These Bedfords were withdrawn from service between February and June 1966, and 294-7/9 were scrapped by a local breaker called Smith. Number 298 lasted a little longer, after it was converted for use as a staff canteen.*

Centre Left: *Some people considered the Bedford chassis to be too light for any real use in heavy stage carriage service work, but a few municipal undertakings did run OBs and SBs. Where the SB found favour was on the lightly loaded rural runs, from country to town, and also school service work. They were cheap to buy and inexpensive to run, but hardly the most attractive vehicles. A representative view is seen in this Duple Midland service bus (WNT 243) dating from 1961 .*

Bottom Left: *There were some improvements to the Duple Midland service body, and here we see a 1965 version which features a roof peak, but it still has the cumbersome arrangement of a door behind the front axle meaning that the driver (if one-manning) would have to turn round almost 180 degrees to collect the fares. The biggest problem with this type of body was its light (all-metal) construction, which endured the perennial problems of condensation and rust.*

It seems as though Duple and Bedford may have come to some arrangement regarding service bus bodies, as both Mulliner and Willowbrook seemed to take up the mantle. Duple were selling the Vega coach so well, that it had all its work cut out to meet the demand. As with the OB Vista, SMT built the Vega body under licence, as did the Loughborough-based company Brush, who came to Duple's aid when a strike at Hendon threatened to interrupt supplies.

Within a year of introduction other bodybuilders were offering their 'wares' on the new SB chassis, and once again we have the benefit of another Bedford brochure for reference. Plaxton were well ahead of the crowd, and they had their 33-seat offering out by mid-1951, although it did resemble the Duple model slightly. Thurgood, however improved matters by offering a 35-seat coach or 37-seat bus, on an extended SB chassis. Other various body styles later included luxury coaches in the 31-35 seat range by the Arlington Motor Co, Gurney Nutting, Churchill and a whole host of smaller builders.

However, in addition to these small concerns, four other significant builders were to begin bodying the SB as serious challengers to both Duple and Plaxton. These firms were Yeates of Loughborough, Harrington of Hove, Willowbrook of Loughborough, and Burlingham. Consequently the SB's success was assured, but we might quote just one example to show how well it was received. Shortly after the launch of the new Bedford at the Commercial Motor Show at Earls Court in London, SMT (Scotland's main Bedford dealer) signed a £1,500,000 (£24,600,000) order for Duple Vega models on SB chassis.

To meet these challenges, in the spring of 1952, Duple's original design was extended some 18 inches (45.7cm) by lengthening the rear overhang of the body, and widened to the now legally allowed 8-foot (2.43m). This led to the fitting of two extra seats for the same purchase price, bringing seating capacity for the new Duple Super Vega body to 36/37 seats. Rear luggage capacities ranged from 80 to 86 cu ft with destination indicators situated either below the front grille, or in two Perspex panels in the canopy. There was also a choice of either two double opening Perspex roof vents or, if preferred, a sliding roof panel, and five different options of exterior moulding schemes to suit individual operators' liveries. These were charged as extra on the Vega, but no extra charge was made on the Super Vega model.

However, the next big change came in time for the 1953 Commercial Motor Show, when Vauxhall launched the 'New Big Bedford Passenger Range'. This was outlined in a new brochure (B594/10/53). Both this brochure and the show stand publicity offered buyers:-
'The Best Of Both Worlds' - 'The Big Bedford passenger chassis is now engineered for diesel as well as for petrol power.'

The diesel and petrol chassis were built on the same assembly line, so apart from the obvious differences in petrol and diesel operation, everything else was common between the two models. As an option to Bedford's own 300cu inch petrol unit, the 108bhp Perkins diesel engine was introduced on the entire S range of bus and truck chassis in response to a growing demand from Bedford customers who wanted diesel-powered engines.

An extra heavy-duty clutch was fitted, together with newly designed air ducts to improve cooling. The starting and lighting system fitted to the diesel model was 24-volt, as opposed to the 12-volt system on the petrol variant, and a vacuum exhauster was fitted to operate the brake servo. Double-acting shock absorbers were introduced front and rear with 8.25x20 10-ply tyres being fitted as standard. Chassis design on the SB included a lower rear level over the arch above the rear axle which was splayed out towards the rear of the vehicle. A 26-gallon fuel tank was fitted. The chassis now came in two weights, with petrol variants being 2$\frac{1}{2}$-tons and diesel 2-tons 14-cwt.

Top Right: *Countless naval men must have passed under the famous archway entrance to Chatham Dockyard and more than a few of them will have done it in this 36-seater Mulliner-bodied Bedford dating from April 1956. Along with four other Bedfords, 1282 RN had a busy time ferrying ratings between ships and the naval barracks or transporting dockyard workers.*

Centre Right: *This is an SB with the Mulliner Mighty Master 32-seat special airport steel-framed body. Used on services to London Airport, PXE 96 was fitted with passengers doors on both sides of the body.*

Bottom Right: *This angular-looking service bus body on KUX 435 was basically a Duple MkV Service Bus body, but was actually built under licence by Mulliner for Phillips of Wrexham, as the Hendon factory were exceptionally busy with coach body orders.*

Top Left: *Whilst Duple were very busy with coach bodies, to the extent that they 'farmed out' service bus bodywork to other builders (before buying Willowbrook and forming Duple Midland), Plaxton did not have the best of times with the Bedford chassis initially. In fact there had been considerable dissent between Vauxhall and Plaxton when the SB was launched in 1950, and the chassis-maker's chosen builder was firmly Duple. However, common sense prevailed and soon Plaxton were offering the Venturer body on the SB chassis. Here we have a 35-seat example (SMB 20 for Altrincham Motorways) seen on Marine Drive, Scarborough, before delivery in March 1954.*

Centre Left: *This is the de-luxe version of the Plaxton Venturer with roof quarter lights and front roof panels. This particular SB (WHT 816) is No.3 in the Coachways (Bristol CWS?) fleet, and it is seen making the assault on the Cheddar Gorge.*

Bottom Left: *After the Venturer, Plaxton launched the Consort (see picture page 3), and then the Embassy body. These models found favour both as coaches and dual-purpose buses. In 1961 Barton No.873, a SB-Embassy (873 HAL) is seen on a Stamford service in front of an Eastern Counties-Bristol (HBD 633) en-route to Corby.*

The SB, like it's predecessor the OB, was to prove such a huge success, that it would continue in production (although with many variants and changes in designation), through to the end of the Bedford era. Indeed by the end of 1978, some 28-years after it's initial concept, 52,000 SB chassis units had been sold, with many going to overseas markets. Engineering changes and improvements came in many guises, all of which will soon be covered in a 112-page history of the Bedford SB by Martin Perry, soon to be published in the **Nostalgia Road Premier Series**.

However, for the moment it is perhaps better for me to concentrate on the emergence of the other major coachbuilders who began bodying the SB in the early 1950s. Of course each of these companies introduced their own progressive improvements as the SB chassis developed, and many of these changes are shown in the pictures that follow, but the 1953-4 catalogue was the first major step that Vauxhall took towards promoting the wares of other body builders.

It was clear that a major alliance still existed with Duple, and the cover of the brochure featured an artist's impression of the Vega with the oval grill, and this was also the first coach body to be shown inside the publication. But as would be expected, Plaxton were also included (on pages 10 and 11), with their Venturer Super Luxury Coach. Seating was for 35 to 37, and it came in a choice of two widths (7-foot 6-inches or 8-foot); the overall length being 29-foot 2-inches (8.89m).

The Venturer body featured luxury 'Dunlopillo' seats, tubular foot rails, highly polished garnish rails and mouldings, with 'cigarette-proof Formica window cappings. Optional extras included roof quarter lights, blister lights to roof corners, Perspex roof vents and roof dome panels. Other extras included, underfloor heaters, carpeting front and rear heater/de-mister units, tubular parcel racks and Radiomobile radio/P.A.

Above: *On pages six and seven of the 1953-4 catalogue there came the Riviera Super Luxury by Yeates. This was a 35- to 38-seat coach that was very light and airy, and finished in a vast amount of polished aluminium. Body width was either 7-foot 6-inches or 8-foot and the overall length 29-foot 2-inches. It had an extensive range of optional extras including large Perspex panels in the front and rear roof domes, glass roof quarter lights, tubular luggage racks, Radiomobile radio and three speakers, an amplification-public address system and rear heaters/demisters. This Riviera SBG (KAY 300) was seen at the 1953 Commercial Motor Show and then went to Olivers Luxicoaches of Loughborough in December 1953.*

Right: *As stated in the text, Yeates modified the SB chassis, to allow one-man-operation by fitting a front entrance door ahead of the axle. That design was named the Fiesta. Here we a further development by the company in the shape of the Yeates Pegasus. As proclaimed by the advert on the windscreen this demonstrator also achieved the grand total of 44-seats. In my home area, G.W Castle and Baddeley Brothers (both of Holmfirth) operated this model!*

Top Left: *As mentioned elsewhere Yeates of Loughborough designed a front-entrance 44-seat version body to fit the SB chassis. In the trio of pictures on this page we have some of the photographs submitted to Vauxhall to prove that the FE44 was a worthwhile concept to pursue. They feature Yeates coach version called the Europa, and here we see 5107 NK before it entered service with Ronsway in March 1961.*

Centre Left: *The second view of the SB8 shows the driver's position or what is described as the 'cockpit view', with all the controls and driver-operated door lever just behind the handbrake.*

Bottom Left: *This is what all the fuss was about, the front entry SB.*

As stated overleaf, Yeates of Loughborough produced some very distinctive bodywork on the SB chassis, and this was to continue on through several variants. To some the Yeates styling was unorthodox and foreign-looking. Some said it had a Continental fashion, others thought it trans-Atlantic, but I leave it to you to look at the photographs and decide which. By the end of the 1950s, Yeates were looking at a new market for the SB, and they proposed either extending the chassis forward of the front axle or moving the axle backwards. The desire was not so much to create a longer bus, but the need to create an economical front-entry chassis that could be used for one man operation.

As shown overleaf, the Pegasus was the first stage in what was called the FE44 project (front-entrance/44-seats), but another 'progression' came with the Europa. This model is seen in the trio of 1961 'publicity pictures' on the left of this page, the same forward 'extension' was employed to good effect to create a 'luxury coach' on the SB chassis. The modification was achieved by moving the front axle backwards, thus allowing for a door and set of steps to be fixed ahead of it.

Vauxhall were quite reluctant to allow this modification, and these fears were proved correct when the Yeates bodies began breaking up behind the drivers seat. The problem was that the SB's front end was not designed to support all the weight of the engine, driver and door so failure was inevitable. A large number of Bedford customers began to complain, but parent company Vauxhall could refute the compensation claims because the modification was not officially approved.

Yeates argued their corner quite forcibly, and thus was proposed a challenge that the FE44 would undertake an endurance run from London to Moscow and back to London in 1961. However, this run was was actually completed in an SB-Yeates Fiesta (YBD 1), but the whole story behind this change of vehicle has been lost in the mists of time.

Although this change of model did nothing to prove that the modification was safe, it is understood that other endurance trials were held with a prototype coach and when the body was taken off the chassis, the extension showed no signs of damage or fatigue. However this whole episode did go on to influence Bedford design policy in the future, and as a consequence the Bedford VAM was produced in response to the operators' demands for a mid-range, front-entry bus or coach chassis. This employed modified SB frames and the front end of the TK truck, and was thus an interesting development of the SB.

Mind you, Yeates were not the only ones offering a bigger coach on the SB, for in 1953 the Blackpool-based firm of H. V Burlingham joined the fray with a smaller version of their Seagull body. Although the Seagull had been well received on the Leyland Royal Tiger chassis, several people thought it too cumbersome to adapt for a smaller chassis like the SB. Tony Anstruther recalls the events, saying 'The MD of Burlingham saw the SB at the 1950 show and said "Bedford really have something for the small operator there." It was decided that we would see if we could design our new luxury coach body to fit the SB, and we got an operator to purchase a Duple Vega on an SB for us. We had them road test the coach for us all through the summer of 1951, and then proceeded to dismantle it back at Blackpool. It appeared in January with a Burlingham body that was light enough not to over-tax the 300cubic inch engine, but was still durable and solid. It used many parts from our Seagull body, and was to become known by many as the Baby Seagull. As it was all-metal construction we had to adapt the frame jigs, but once this was done we knew we could build a 35-seat coach without any problems. Now, whilst several of our competitors were looking at upgrading a small chassis to carry more seats, we were doing the opposite. After all we already had a good maximum capacity model with our centre entrance Seagull, but we knew that there was a certain market each year for a number of small coaches that combined luxury with roominess. As a consequence we produced the Seagull 'armchair' model, which would accommodate just 31 passengers.'

Production standards on the Burlingham models were very high indeed, and as a result the list of optional equipment was limited to items like Clayton Heaters (one each side) KL combined de-froster and de-mister), glass roof quarter lights, Perspex roof panels in the sliding, lift-up or fixed roof, Triplex glass front roof domes, Sundyn twin fog lamps and a four-speaker radio/PA system. As if to show the popularity of the new SB range, there were no fewer than five new SB-based vehicles on show at the SMT showrooms at the time of the Scottish Motor Show in Glasgow in 1954. By 1955 Bedford were domineering in both entry list, and indeed prize list in the first British Coach Rally, which was held at Clacton-on-Sea in April.

Top Right: *Here we have what has to be one of the most luxurious bodies ever put on a Bedford in the 1950s, with the SBG Burlingham Seagull. This 36-seat coach entered service with Transglobe Tours (Bread Street, Birmingham 1) in April 1954. Registered OOA 735 it became their fleet number three.*

Centre Right: *An interior view of Transglobe's No.3 showing the superb accommodation from front to back.*

Bottom Right: *Look at it another way, rear to front, and you will see why this is my editor's favourite bus. He travelled to school on a Burlingham Seagull with Baddeley Brothers, and I recall those operated by Wallace Arnold. We would dearly like to preserve one of these Burlingham Seagull coaches, so if you know of one tucked away somewhere, give us a call at Trans-Pennine.*

Top Left: *What followed by the Blackpool-based builder was not quite as inspiring as the early Seagull. We now have variations on a theme firstly with a Burlingham Seagull 61, 51 BXR. This SB8 was fleet number 1718 with H.J. Phillips & Son, and the legal lettering shows its address as London SW1. This model has a roof box destination blind and dates from 1961-2.*

Centre Left: *Next comes (572 BYE) for Pan American, which has a bumper bar destination blind and a rear luggage compartment.*

Bottom Left: *This SB1 Seagull 60 C41F (829 ENN), was new in 1960 and is seen on a service to Stamford in Lincolnshire in February 1961. As number 829 in the Barton fleet this was one of a batch of vehicles purchased for a dual purpose role. During the week they would be employed on stage carriage services, but at weekends and evenings they were used for excursions, tour and private hire work and as such were fitted out to full coach specification.*

In late summer of 1955, Bedford announced a larger version of the SB chassis. By increasing the wheelbase 10-inches to a new length of 216-inches (5.5m) the new chassis could now accommodate luxury bodywork of up to 41 seating capacity, and to the then legally allowed maximum 30-foot (9.1m) overall length. The 300cu-inch petrol engine was by this time giving 115bhp, with the Perkins 108bhp R6 continuing as the diesel alternative. The petrol chassis variant in 1955 cost £855 (£11,115), but purchase tax was only payable on units used for non-psv work. Yet, because many bus chassis were used for 'specialist' bodies, ie: mobile showrooms, horseboxes, travelling surgeries, x-ray vans and mobile libraries etc, so several SBs fell into this trap.

Due to increasing productivity of both Vauxhall cars and the ever growing commercial range, a further expansion plan costing £36 million (£468,000,000) was announced. This in turn led to the first Bedford chassis being produced at a new truck and bus plant in Dunstable on 2nd August 1955. Once again engine designs were improved, and in Spring 1957 another diesel option became available in the form of the Leyland 0.350 unit. This was designated the SB8 and had 6-cylinders with a capacity of 5.76 litres. Much more important at this time though, was Bedford's announcement of their own 300cu inch diesel engine in February 1957. This was Bedford's first home-built diesel engine, designed for certain truck chassis, but also available on the SB early in 1958. This was a 300cu inch vertical 6-cylinder 4-stroke unit of 4.93 litres capacity, which developed 97bhp at 2,800 rpm, and was designated SB1. As you may notice the once simple designation system of the early days were (by now) getting slightly complicated.

The Perkins variant had become the SBO (oil) when fitted in 1953, with the petrol variant becoming known as the SBG (gasoline). Another option at this time was the availability of a two-speed rear axle. On the introduction of the SB8 (Leyland engine), the SBG was re-designated the SB3. Shortly after the introduction of Bedford's diesel unit on the SB chassis in 1958, the fitting of Perkins engines was discontinued and production of the SBO ceased.

On May 28th 1958 the one millionth Bedford was produced, a staggering fact when you consider that the firm was still only 27 years old. Furthermore, of this number, 360,000 had been sold to the export market. Three years were to lapse before the next major change was to be announced in the SB's life, when in December 1961, a larger Bedford-built 6-cylinder engine was introduced as a replacement for the SB1. This unit was a 330cu inch diesel with a capacity of 5.42 litres and designated SB5. Further alterations included hydraulically-operated air brakes, a choice of either 4- or 5-speed synchromesh gearbox, and single or two-speed rear axle and these were made available on both the SB5 and SB8 chassis. In 1963 the Leyland O.370 engine was fitted as opposed to the earlier 0.350 unit, and the SB8 was discontinued in favour of the newer engine which was designated SB13.

In August 1965 the new VAM range was announced, but between its launch in 1950 and 1965 over 29,000 SB units had been produced. The SB continued in production, despite the addition of the new VAM chassis; unlike it's predecessor the OB, the SB was still finding favour in certain quarters of the market. With only the SB13 model being dropped from production, the SB soldiered on, although re-designated (again), as SB (NJM) and available in less quantities. The final stage of development saw a revised wheelbase to 18-feet (5.5m), and had the options of either Bedford's own 5.4 diesel unit, or their 4.93 litre petrol engine. The SB became a popular choice for the armed forces, both at home and abroad of which most were bodied by Mulliner.

The SB story does not end here, and we have only been able to give a brief insight into what is a remarkable and un-written history of a popular bus chassis. Yet this a matter that we will put to rights in the not too distant future, with a book especially on the subject. In Britain a handful of SBs remain in service, some are preserved (but not as many as the OB/OWB), a few have been converted into travelling homes or car transporters, and some that are still in use as greenhouses or garden sheds. One of these vehicles that survived as a garden shed is ex-Potteries Motor Traction SB5/Yeates Pegasus DP45F (951 UVT), which has just been rescued from the Shetland Islands by a group of enthusiasts from the Midlands.

Top Right: *Another smaller builder on the SB was Strachans who produced the Everest luxury coach body. Here we see 456 EMC supplied for continental work with Motorways, 85 Knightsbridge SW1.*

Centre Right: *Thomas Harrington of Hove also built on a number of SB chassis, and here we have their show model pictured in November 1960 prior to the Commercial Motor Show at Earls Court.*

Bottom Right: *This SB5 is a good example of an 'export' order. In 1968, EZL 160 was one of 545 Bedford school buses to enter service with CIE (Ireland's national transport authority), after the government decreed that free school transport had to be provided nationally. Hundreds of buses were needed almost overnight and Bedford sent the chassis for assembly by their distributors McCairns Motors, whilst the bodies were built in CIE's Dublin workshops.*

This final part of the SB story is something I wanted to spend a few moments talking about, although it does not really belong in a bus book at all. I am talking about buses that weren't actually buses, in other words those SB chassis that were supplied for bodying in non-PSV applications. As I mentioned earlier, there were quite a lot of these 'specials' and the use for the SB chassis varied widely both at home and abroad. The three pictures on this page give some idea of how its use varied, but they form only the tip of the iceberg. In a future book in the **Nostalgia Road** series I want to look at the use of PSV chassis used in non-PSV work, and I would take this opportunity for enthusiasts with any knowledge of building, use and application to contact me care of the publishers. Photograph and builders specification details would be particularly useful. For the moment Trans-Pennine are looking at the subject in another **Nostalgia Road** book on *Britain's Mobile Libraries*, and I can give a sneak preview and tell readers that quite a few SBs will be featured in that book.

Libraries were just one use, horseboxes were another, as both applications found use for a chassis that gave a low floor height and thus allowed easy access for both humans and animals. This obviated the need to climb to the higher levels of floor that came from the use of a conventional truck chassis, and whilst the SB was nothing new in low floor height (AEC and Leyland had made low chassis for years) the big difference was that Bedford chassis were cheaper. As many of the applications came under nationalised services (X-ray units) or local authority social/welfare budgets (mobile libraries, fire engines) the price was a major factor. In other words, if the councils could not buy a vehicle at the right price, the service may not have been provided. The horse-racing fraternity (especially those engaged in farming) found that the SB was cheap enough to provide an 'exclusive' horsebox instead of using other farm vehicles. No longer did farmer Giles have to baulk at the thought of buying an AEC or Maudslay chassis for the horsebox that his daughter wanted, he could now look at a good combination of Bedford and Jennings or Vincent and the like. The SB didn't quite have 1,001 uses, but with fire engines and ambulances it did have 999.

Top Left: *This Duple Vega bodied SB (RKX 337) was pictured in 1953 at Stoke Mandeville Hospital. This specially-adapted coach carried wheel-chair patients from the hospital, and had three forms of access. There was a conventional nearside front door behind the front axle, this ramp behind the driver's seat on the off-side, and a double door with hydraulic tail-lift at the rear.*

Centre Left: *This mobile bank, built on a 206-inch wheelbase SB chassis, was used by the Standard Bank of South Africa, to provide the facilities of a modern bank to customers in outlying areas in the Cape Peninsula. The spacious body was built by Messrs J Brockhouse (SA) Limited of Cape Town and the chassis was supplied by Williams, Hunt & Johnston Limited, Vauxhall and Bedford dealers in that city.*

Bottom Left: *Underneath this Australian mobile television transmitting vehicle is a 1951 SB chassis - honestly.*

Above: *As will be seen from our cover picture, Bedford SBs were well liked in the Shetland Islands, but it is strange that two near consecutively registered SB-Vegas arrived at different times with different operators. Like KWX 412, this West Riding-registered coach (KWX 440) was painted in a blue and cream livery when it arrived in the islands. However, this particular vehicle was operated by Petersons of Ollaberry in the North Mainland. New to Balme of Otley in August 1951, it arrived in Shetland in 1959 and is seen here in Lerwick bus station in the 1960s.* Ken Jubb

Left: *Many enthusiasts will remember the distinctive red, green and cream livery employed by Vaggs of Shropshire. Here a 1952 Bedford SB-Duple Vega (MXB 504), stands at their Knockin Heath Depot. The picture dates from the spring of 1972, when the SB is seen in the company of contemporary members of the fleet including an ex-Yelloway Harrington-bodied AEC and a later Bedford SB with a Duple Super Vega body.* Martin Perry

Above: *This second Shetland colour picture again shows another Bedford with Petersons, this time an SB3 with a Duple Vega C41F body. Originally registered in Lancashire in 1956, it was acquired by Petersons in 1962 and was sold to H. Wood in 1966. A full history of bus operations in these northern islands is given in our 164-page book* Shetland Buses In The 20th Century, *which contains 640 pictures, 432 in full colour. Gordon M. Jamieson*

Left: *This view offers an interesting comparison of two major British coachbuilders. On the left stands 6055 PT a 1961, 330 diesel-engined SB1 with Plaxton Embassy coachwork, which had been supplied new to Rennisons of Hartburn, Co. Durham. On the right is TVJ 137, a 1959 300 petrol-powered SB3 with a Duple Super Vega body. It was new to Yeomans-Miller of Hereford and was latterly with WEMS of Weston-super-Mare. At the time this picture was taken both coaches were in service with Beeline of Warminster. Martin Perry*

Above: *Like the coach opposite, 8193 TE was also supplied new to a Lancashire operator, this time Woods Coaches of Ashton-under-Lyne. This 1963 vehicle demonstrates its ability to move 52 passengers at once - a hitherto unheard of figure for a Bedford PSV. This was actually the 55th Plaxton body to be built on the new twin-steer Bedford VAL14 chassis (chassis number 1094). It is seen here in Halesowen (West Midlands), possibly whilst carrying workers from the British Motor Corporation factory (Austin) at Longbridge, but the operator is not recorded. Note the 1967-registered Hillman Imp van following the coach as it passes through the town. Martin Perry*

Right: *Basking in the Mid-Wales sunshine, KCJ 185E was a 330 diesel-engined VAM5 fitted with Duple Viscount 45-seat bodywork. New in 1967 to Sargeants of Kington, she was in service with Selwyn Hughes of Llanfair Caereinion when photographed in the summer of 1972. Martin Perry*

Above: *With their attractive two-tone green livery, the long-established business of Warners of Tewksbury were good Bedford customers during the 1950s, '60s and '70s. This scene at their depot offers a comparison between Bedford-Duple offerings in the 1960s. On the left is a (then) new 1968 Bedford VAM70 with a Duple Viceroy C45F body. On the right, and seven years its senior, is 5664 DD, an SB5 with a 41-seat Duple Super Vega body. The livery shown here is not dissimilar to the colour scheme that I am progressively painting the Trans-Pennine fleet of Bedford coaches.* Martin Perry

Left: *For the 1969 touring season, one of the smallest National Bus Company operators, United Welsh, took delivery of a pair 45-seat Bedford VAMs with the re-styled Duple Viceroy bodywork. Once again seen under a flawless sky with bright sunshine, we see fleet number 22 (PCY 985G). The picture is taken at the Western Welsh depot in St. Davids during the summer of 1970.* Martin Perry

THE SB CARRIES ON

The SB didn't end with the close of the 1960s, in fact it was available to the end of bus and truck production, but by then it had been designated the Bedford NJM. This later offering looked very attractive with the Plaxton Panorama IV or the Duple Dominant body, both of which had a pair of seats in front of the entry door. In the mid-1960s hundreds of SBs were produced with two principle types of body, namely the Panorama and the Bella Vega (as shown above). The latter was later replaced by the Duple Vega 31 in 1969, as the new Duple-SB offering for the early 1970s, but the days of coach production at Hendon were numbered and the work would soon be transferred to the former Burlingham plant at Blackpool.

Above: *Typical of the SB development in the first half of the 1960s was this Duple Bella Vega C41F (21 JBM). It entered service with Buckmaster Coaches in 1963, and the picture is taken in 1964.*

The SB held its own for over 20 years at the top of the field, and it continued steadily for another 10 years, although the market was declining in favour of more modern designs. Even so, it has to be one of the longest production runs of any coach chassis anywhere in the world. The story is far too complex to cover in detail here, but the publishers have asked me to use this space to appeal to readers for any anecdotal information, service histories or photographs for use in Martin Perry's forthcoming definitive history on the subject.

THE SMALL BEDFORDS

Up until the emergence of the celebrated 'Big Bedford' SB chassis in 1950, Bedford had always been regarded as a strictly small-size chassis producer. Indeed as mentioned previously in this book, the early Bedford range were not buses at all, merely truck chassis adapted to serve the role. In some cases their passenger vehicles were simply unaltered commercial chassis that entered public service with bus bodies fitted on them. Back then there were various coachbuilders who would undertake all manner of adaptations, but by the end of World War II much of the variety had vanished completely. But Vauxhall were still offering a factory built small bus. In fact Luton began to offer a vehicle with a 'factory-built' bus body as early as 1932. Using what was originally intended as a delivery van, they marketed the 'Rural Bus'.

As mentioned in our companion book, *Bedford Buses of the 1930s & '40s* this was a seven-seat vehicle, designated the VYC. It had a 106-inch wheelbase, and the 16.9hp engine that was at the time being used to power the Vauxhall Cadet saloon. As the years progressed, Bedford concentrated more on larger chassis, such as the WLB, and eventually the more important and much favoured OB design.

Even so there was still a market for vehicles of 20-seats or less. To this end Bedford modified their M series of goods chassis in order to appease those customers who still had no need for a larger vehicle. Along with the OB, the ML chassis was first introduced in 1939. It had a 143-inch (3.6m) wheelbase, the Bedford 28hp petrol engine, and used the same basic components as the OB. Despite the inevitable cessation of production brought about by emergence of World War II, this chassis was re-introduced at the end of 1945.

Top Left: *The archetypal minibus is found in this obviously posed publicity shot of a Bedford CA Dormobile Conversion, showing a split-screen short wheel based model (WKM 413) in 1956.*

Top Right: *Here we have an earlier (and slightly more basic) CA Utility Estate Wagon, built by Kenex. It was known as the Roadmaster and was launched in time for the 1953 Commercial Motor Show, and aimed primarily at contractors and small operators.*

Centre Right: *Next we see a 1960 long wheel base model, the CAL school bus supplied to Attwoods of Perth in Australia. Incredible as it may seem, this was advertised as carrying 24 seats and costing £454.9s.0d (£5,408) plus state tax £68.0s.0d (£810) and this was in Australian pounds, then much lower in value than the British pound.*

Bottom Right: *More traditionally recognised as a British minibus we show the CAL PSV chassis. This particular model features a Dormobile coach (Martin Walter conversion), which boasted greater headroom and better seating than the 'modified' CA van. This view dates from September 1964, but the bodywork does not look particularly dated even now. Few of these CA-Dormobile buses have survived into the 21st-Century, but we know where there is one just begging to be restored, don't we Gordon?*

From 1946 through to 1953, the M Type chassis was frequently made available for conversion with bus bodywork and thus forms the first part of the small bus story in the 1950s and '60s. Another chassis made available at about the same time was the OL, which was modified from the 157-inch (3.99m) wheelbase 3/4-ton truck chassis. These vehicles came with a higher ground clearance to enable them to traverse uneven and poorly maintained roads, and were introduced mainly for the export market. Many were exported to Cyprus and were fitted with locally built dual-purpose bodies, which accommodated passengers on the inside whilst goods were carried on a rear tailboard and on a large carrier fitted to the roof of the vehicle.

A particularly rare adaptation for service-passenger work from Bedford came about in the form of the QL model. These vehicles had a 143-inch (3.63m) wheelbase and were fitted with a 28hp 6-cylinder petrol engine. They also had four-wheel drive and a very high ground clearance as they were built specifically for military use between 1941 and 1945. It was therefore unusual to see these actually in service with bus operators, but as they had a relatively low seating capacity I have included them in this chapter on small buses (despite their obviously serious overall size and weight).

The main operator to use the QL was Southport Corporation, who purchased a batch of 12 such vehicles at a war surplus sale in 1946. These were used in their service across Ainsdale Beach from 1947 onwards, after they had been completely overhauled and converted to 23-seat single-deck configuration by bodybuilders Rimmer, Harrison & Sutherland. The last of these vehicles remained in service at Southport until 1966.

Top Left: *This Bedford A Type (130 GMC), with a 12-seater Spurling crew car body, was operated by British European Airways at Glasgow and used to convey crews from Prestwick airport to city hotels and return. Seen here on 2nd May 1958, it is passing a BEA Pionair Class aircraft named* RMA Frederick Lanchester.

Centre Left: *Another A Type, this has a Duple 26-seat body and was used by Vauxhall as a Bedford-Duple demonstrator. It had a maximum legal speed of 30mph and an unladen weight of 3-ton 19-cwt. It is pictured in October 1953 just before the Commercial Motor Show.*

Bottom Left: *This 29-seat Duple Vista is shown in MacBraynes fleet list as having a C4Z2 chassis, but Vauxhall's records show it as a C5 chassis from 1958. It had a special moulding scheme and glass roof quarter lights, and was sold to Laidlaw's of Rutherglen in 1969.*

In the early 1950s, although the new SB chassis was once again bringing great success, it was seen that there was still room to expand in the small-chassis market. Again based on the OL chassis, the OLAZ was to prove it's worth in Scotland, where David MacBrayne was a big user of this model, their purchasing no fewer than 22 outside-panelled Sportsman models from Duple who had been unable to sell them elsewhere. The sale was agreed at a 'beneficial price' and Duple added external panelling to the outside framing of the Sportsman. They did not, however, think to fill in the panels at the bottom and over the years dirt and debris filled the void, the screws rusted and the body panels came away. The OLAZ had a wheelbase of 157-inches (3.99m), as opposed to the 174-inches (4.4m) on the OB, so the new model, whilst looking similar from the front view, appeared slightly taller, more "squat", and perhaps even 'dumpier' than the previous OB.

Another chassis to be adapted for carrying bus bodywork following the discontinuation of the OB, was the TA chassis. Based on the TA 4-ton truck chassis and designated TA-A4L, this was used for the fitting of 14- to 18-seat bodywork. (This vehicle was of normal control layout with a wheelbase of 167-inch (4.24m), 4-speed synchromesh gearbox, hypoid final drive and vacuum-servo assisted hydraulic brakes.) There was an option of either the 6-cylinder petrol engine of 3.52 litres, or, alternatively the 4.73 litre diesel unit. Although one or two saw service in this country, most of these vehicles were sold to the overseas market. This model continued in production until its succession by a new model in February 1957.

Mid-1957 saw another chassis for the small-coach operator in the form of the C Type 29/30-seat bus chassis. This was based on the 4-ton forward-control truck chassis, of which the smaller versions were derived from the same cab as the forward-control S types. Once again all modifications complied with the PSV legislation of the day, and it was on this chassis that the Vista name (previously used by Duple on the OB) was to re-appear. With a 29-seat capacity, the 4-ton Bedford-Duple Vista/Super Vista, once again sold well. So much so, that after the initial batch of 55 were sold, Duple exhibited this model based on the C4Z1 petrol-engined chassis at the 1958 Commercial Motor Show.

The other designations for this vehicle were C4Z2 for the 4-ton diesel chassis whilst the heavier 5-ton chassis was designated C5Z2. There was also a choice of 7 foot 6 inch or 8 foot vehicle widths available on this model. All versions of this model carried a 4-speed synchromesh gearbox, hypoid rear axle, and vacuum-servo hydraulic brakes. Both the C4Z1 and the heavier C5Z1 were fitted with the Bedford 3.52 litre 6-cylinder petrol engine, whilst the C4Z2 and C5Z2 diesel options carried the 6-cylinder 4.93 litre oil unit. Two other options available designated C4Z3 and C5Z3 were fitted with a 4.93 litre petrol unit of 6-cylinders. The complete C range of chassis remained available until 1961 when Bedford announced the new VAS chassis was to be purpose-built for passenger service use.

Launched in 1958, a new 35-cwt chassis was to mainly find it's popularity not initially in the bus market, but instead as an ambulance chassis, (see our book Famous Fleets Vol.2 *NHS Ambulances-The First Twenty-five Years*). It became known as the J1 type. Even so, the J1 became widely used also by airports as crew-buses, and in this guise they were usually exempt from stringent PSV regulations regarding fare-paying passenger vehicles in force at that time.

Also in the 1950s was the introduction of the 'mini-bus' era, in which Bedford were once again one of the early suppliers. With this new challenge came a host of albeit 'new' body manufacturers. One such supplier was the Folkestone coachbuilders Martin Walter who, in 1952, converted the Bedford CA van into a 7-seater which became known as the Utilavan. This new small-capacity vehicle had a 90-inch (2.28m) wheelbase and carried a 1.5 litre 4-cylinder Vauxhall petrol engine, a 3-speed synchromesh gearbox and was fitted with hydraulic brakes. Layout was of the semi-forward control type. By 1953 Martin Walter had increased the seating capacity to 12, in order to meet the growing demand, but seating often remained very basic and often employed the wooden slatted type of construction used on the OWB service buses. Various marketing names followed it through to 1960, including the Dormobile, and the Utilabus.

Top Right: *This Bedford Duple service bus is an unusual combination as it employs the DLZ chassis. Registered KHR 923 it was used for transport to and from Odstock Hospital, near Salisbury.*

Centre Right: *Elegance in a Bedford TJ? It hardly sounds likely at the first mention, but here is living proof in a body built by Readings of Portsmouth. In this super mini-bus 'Very important passengers' could enjoy real luxury travel. This 12-seater coach on the normal-control 35-cwt Bedford chassis, was light and airy thanks to large windows and eight clear Perspex lights in the roof. The wide, thickly padded seats add to the atmosphere of luxury; so too did the heater, the rich carpeting, and the glove-nets on the backs of the seats.*

Bottom Right: *Exterior fittings on the Reading 12-seat body included fog-lamps, flashing indicators at front and rear, windscreen washers, and chrome-plated bumper and radiator grille. The seating on 577 NTW were twin on the offside and single on the near.*

Above: *The Bedford Coach Rally of 1963 with a J2-Plaxton from Casks Coaches of Patricroft, Manchester, and a Bedford-Plaxton VAL belonging to Price's Coaches in the background.*

Other designs becoming available on the CA chassis by 1959 included the 'Busette', a 12-seat built on the CA model by Marshall of Cambridge. Grosvenor of Watford offered a conversion and so too did Kenex. Then, in 1959, a longer version of the CA became available, and this really boosted the minibus market. To identify the different chassis lengths, the original 90-inch wheelbase CA became the CAS (CA short), whilst the new 102-inch (2.59m) wheelbase version was designated the CAL (CA long). Once again the new vehicle was adapted for 11- to 12-seat bodywork conversion.

By 1961, an alternative drive unit was offered to the original petrol engine. This was the 4-cylinder Perkins diesel of 1.6 litres and drove through a 4-speed synchromesh gearbox. This new gearbox was to supersede the original 3-speed gearbox throughout the range (with the exception of the petrol engined CAS), although the 3-speed box would still be available to special order. The Perkins unit lasted through to the mid-1960s, when it was replaced by a larger 1.76 litre diesel engine.

This was to be the mainstay power unit in the vehicle until the cessation of production of the model in 1968, in preparation of the introduction of the new CF model in 1969. Early versions of this new vehicle had a choice of 3- or 4-speed synchromesh gearbox for the shorter wheelbase (106-inch) model, and were made available with either Bedford's own 1.59 litre 4-cylinder petrol engine, or, if preferred, the Perkins 1.76 litre diesel unit. The longer wheelbase (126-inch) model came equipped with the Bedford 1.98 litre 4-cylinder petrol engine, or again the 2.54 litre Perkins diesel variant. The 4-speed gearbox was standard on all long wheelbase versions of the CF range, but more of this in the next book. As before the layout was semi-forward control, with all models having hydraulic servo-assisted brakes, and a hypoid rear axle.

Another very popular small model from the Bedford stable was the J2 originally dating from around 1958. This was based on the bonneted normal control J2 truck chassis but was modified to a forward control layout either by Bedford, or in many cases by the bodywork supplier. Indeed, some builders merely 'designed' a shorter version of their original larger body designs. One such builder was Plaxton with their Embassy body, which even when scaled down for the smaller J2 vehicle still looked attractive, although the 8-foot wide version looked somewhat uneasy with the narrow-track front wheels. One of Duple's offerings for this chassis was the 'Compact', a very neat 20-seat coach.

As stated previously, the J1 chassis was more popular as an ambulance chassis, following which the J2 had many designations, for its varied usage. The J2S (short wheelbase), and J2L (long wheelbase), were normally converted to forward control, whilst the J3L remained in it's normal-control form. Engine options on the range were the 3.52 litre 6-cylinder petrol unit, or the 4-cylinder 3.14 litre diesel engine. The complete range was fitted with a 4-speed synchromesh gearbox, hydraulic vacuum brakes, and a spiral bevel rear axle. The J2S was available for 20-seat bodywork, whilst the J3L and J4L could seat up to 29 passengers. The original 3.14 litre oil engine was replaced in May 1960, with a larger 3.29 litres oil unit, again with 4-cylinders, and this was later upgraded to 3.61 litres in 1967, although throughout this time there were no alterations made to the petrol variant.

Although out of our time scope, it is however worth noting that in 1974, a special order of four J2 models were built for use in Guernsey. Once again modified to forward control layout and designated J6L, these vehicles had a 179-inch (5.45m) wheelbase, which enabled them to be fitted with 27-foot (8.23m) bodywork. By having an overall width of only 6-foot 11-inch (2.1m), they were able to conform to the limits imposed by Guernsey's authorities.

Again the small coach range is a subject deserving much greater consideration, and it is one that the publishers are looking at covering in much greater depth, but I hope that in these few short pages I have been able to give something of an introduction to the subject.

Top Right: *As stated above, the story of the J2 is deserving of a book in its own right, and remarkably quite a few of these underrated workhorses still survive, so they must have a great appeal. Compared to the Reading body shown earlier, the 19-seat Duple Compact Coach was really rather basic. This 1967-68 J2S demonstrator went to Bletchley Motor Coaches, Buckinghamshire.*

Centre Right: *Despite the rather bland external look of the Duple minibus body, the interior had a more luxurious feel. This example shows a 15-seat body on the J2 chassis. Note the plastic seat backs and the tubular luggage racks. Also worthy of note is the large area of open space on the front near-side of the coach.*

Bottom Right: *Moving on to 1960, here we have an 'artist's impression' of the slightly larger J4 chassis with a Duple metal framed 30-seater bus body.*

THE VAS SERIES

The Bedford VAS was another new offering for the 1960s, and one that went some considerable way to recapturing ground that had been traditional Bedford territory since the days of the 29-seat OB. In fact you could say it was the return of the small bus to suit traditional Bedford operators, who had found that the SB had been getting progressively bigger whilst their passenger loadings had not. By the start of the 1960s, the national fleet of OBs were becoming quite dated and although the OB would last quite a while longer in some areas, many operators were demanding something new of Bedford.

The planning began in 1959, and by 1961 Vauxhall were able to announce the return of a 29-/31-seat chassis. Named the VAS (VA Short), it would have a wheelbase of 164-inches (4.16m), and a low height that would be achieved with a new feature from Bedford - 16-inch (40cm) road wheels. Funnily enough, when transport authorities are craving for easy-access, low-floor-height buses in the 21st Century, it is ironic to note that the VAS partially solved the problem 40-years earlier simply by fitting smaller wheels.

Top Left: *In this superb publicity photograph, we see a winning combination for the coach operator of the 1960s. Just the thing with which to replace their aging OB, was the Duple Bella Vista C29F body on the VAS chassis. Dating from 1964 we see 260 MTM 2 a Bella Vista Duple on VAS chassis for Eddie's Coaches.*

Bottom Left: *Just to prove that they are still around, here we have BJX 848C - new to Abbeyways of Halifax in 1965. I am pictured with the coach at Jamieson's Garage, Cullivoe, Isle of Yell, Shetland in April 2000, just prior to moving it to Trans-Pennine of Appleby.*

Top Right: *Next we see a VAS with the Plaxton Embassy body registration 8000 MD. It was new to Bloomfield's Worldwide Coaches Limited, Camberwell Road, London (on hire to Trafalgar Tours, London for touring the USA with Miss Great Britain) and is pictured outside Earls Court Commercial Motor Show in 1962.*

Centre Right: *This diagram shows the original prototype short wheel base VAS coach chassis. Dated 16th May 1961 it shows an SB-like scuttle and cowl.*

Bottom Right: *Another Bedford VAS, this time what we think was a regular Vauxhall demonstrator (10 EPE). It is seen in company with another Plaxton-bodied coach (SB-Consort) registered 715 ANM owned by Diadem Coaches.*

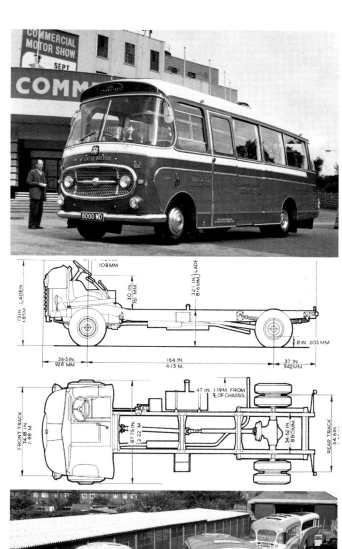

Two models of this forward-control chassis were available, these being designated VAS1 (fitted with the Bedford 300cu 6-cylinder diesel engine) and the VAS2 (which had the Bedford 214cu 6-cylinder petrol engine). The VAS1 had hydraulic operated air brakes, whilst the VAS2 had vacuum-servo assisted hydraulic brakes. Both models had a transmission handbrake that acted on the prop shaft, a device which I personally did not like. Transmissions on both early models was by a 4-speed gearbox driving through a spiral bevel rear axle.

In 1962 engine improvements made the news, when Vauxhall announced the new Bedford 220 and 330 power units as an option for the existing 200 and 300 units. Shortly after this, the 300 (used mostly for bus and coach application in the SB) was dropped.

By 1967 the VAS1 had become the VAS5, and there was an option for a 5-speed gearbox on this diesel-engined model. Progressive development of the VAS continued over the years, and the model remained (with many changes) in production for quite some considerable time. It eventually became known as the Bedford PJK, but many operators still refer to their vehicles by the original designation.

The concept of re-introducing a small, light-weight chassis was just what the market needed, and the VAS held its price even when secondhand. As an example, it is quite remarkable to state that when Gordon Jamieson bought BJX 848C in 1969, he paid £129 (£1,037) more for the vehicle than Abbeyways had paid for it new in 1965 - in the meantime the coach had done a year with Abbeyways and three years with Warren's of Neath, South Wales.

Top and Centre Left: *Not the most elegant of design combinations, but nevertheless an inexpensive and reliable small bus was formed in this marriage of the VAS and the Duple Midland B28F body. It was, at 3-tons 19-cwt, a lightweight combination and ideal for many rural applications. Here we see MacBraynes No.191 (AYS 737B), which was new in 1964. Although taken in monochrome, these pictures readily show the layout of the attractive apple green, cream, and red livery applied to this operator's fleet. They also illustrate the Royal Route emblem beside the passenger door. Although the body designation is shown as being a service bus, the seats look to be of dual purpose pattern, with deep padded moquette and chrome-plated grab-handles acting as head rests. This particular VAS was later sold to another Scottish operator, Highland Omnibus where it became Fleet No. CD56 on acquisition in 1970.*

Bottom Left: *This 1964 Bedford VAS carries a Duple Midland B30F body, but had the slightly lower unladen weight of 3-tons 18-cwt despite the extra pair of seats. It was owned by Turnberry Hotel, and carried the registration plate AGE 562B.*

Bodywork on the VAS came from a variety of makers, but one of the front runners was Duple, and they instantly hit on the idea of using a name associated with OB to help promote their wares. Recalling the Vista name, they christened their latest offering the Bella Vista (beautiful view). It was, and still is, a surprisingly modern looking coach, and had a flair that was common through the new Duple range. Yet out of the three offerings, the Bella Vega, Vega Major and the Bella Vista, the latter had a certain something that escapes description. Perhaps it was because this was the first really modern-looking small bus to emerge, or maybe it was because it was such a contrast with the OB-Duple Vista that was still in such widespread use in the 1960s. It did the same job as the OB-Vista, the economies of operation were not much different, but in design it was light-years ahead.

When we brought BJX 848C out of retirement at Cullivoe, and took it for display at the Shetland Classic Car Show (the most northerly vehicle rally in Britain) the public's reaction varied greatly. There were those who recognised the Bella Vista as being a 35-year old coach, but equally there were many who thought that it was 'too modern' to be on display at an event like that.

Plaxton, on the other hand developed their Embassy coach model, and whilst it looked nice at the time of introduction, the coaching press were saying it had a dated feel about it by the late 1960s. Yet the Plaxton small coach offering went on well into the 1970s, and several have been preserved. The VAS-Plaxton combination was also favoured by many local authorities, and several were used by Social Services departments and ambulance brigades for transporting disabled patients to/from hospital or local day-care centres. One such vehicle, now preserved by the editor of *Vintage Commercial Vehicle* magazine, Brian Gooding, was a Bedford J2 with the Plaxton body. This coach-ambulance (LAK 118G) was purchased at a time when Bradford Corporation were unable to get the VAS chassis due to high demand.

What happened at Bradford in the late-1960s highlights what was happening nationally, as there was a growing list of operators wanting to acquire the VAS at a time when Bedford and their coachbuilders were falling behind on delivery. Adequate supplies of the J-type were coming through and some of these were offered in lieu of the VAS, but in many applications the loaded bodywork was too heavy for the chassis. This led to a few warranty problems, but even so the Plaxton body has lasted on both types of chassis. Plaxton also offered a 33-seat body for an extended or 'stretched' VAS chassis. Even so it was not just the big two British coachbuilders that were making use of the VAS, and a variety of builders made offerings for this chassis. Yet, the number of British coachbuilders were rapidly diminishing, so it was something of a surprise to see a firm more commonly associated with fire engines, Anglo Bodybuilders of Batley, designing a school bus on the VAS chassis in 1969. In fact, quite a number of builders were making school-bus bodies for the VAs in the late 1960s, including Marshall of Cambridge. They had already enjoyed quite favourable reviews of their service bus body for the VAS back in the mid-1960s, which was called the Cambrette. As one of the pictures on this page show, the Marshall-bodied VAS service bus found favour in Coventry where it was used on rail link and shopper's services. Indeed, one ventures to suggest that the VAS was really one of the earliest 'Hoppa' buses, although it may not be automatically recognised as such. Duple of course were still bashing out the Midland service bus body, but they would make an improvement to the coach variant in the Autumn of 1965 with the Vista 25, which reflected the increased length of 25-feet.

Before long other exotic bodies began to appear on the VAS in the shape of the Moseley Continental Sintra, whilst on the continent the chassis was well-liked by Belgian builders Van Hool. The VAS was a perfect complement to its bigger brothers the VAM and the VAL, and it filled a much-needed gap in the market place. They were also superb to both drive and work on, a fact that I can well appreciate!

Top Right: *This was the 30-seat all-metal Duple Midland service bus body mounted to the Bedford VAS chassis. It was advertised as having 'Full Depth sliders if required.'*

Centre Right: *This 1964 Bedford VAS has an early Cambrette body by Marshall of Cambridge. The all-metal 29-seater (B29F) bus body had an unladen weight of 4-tons 3-cwt, and this particular example (3255 PJ) was owned by Brown Motor Services, of Forest Green.*

Bottom Right: *Registration numbers CRW 503C and CRW 507C were part of a batch of Marshall Cambrette all-metal bus bodies ordered by Coventry City Transport. They were used on a rail-bus link service in the city, and although designed for one-man-operated pay as you enter duties on route 25 (from Station Pool Meadow), they did carry conductors on some duties. Here we see 503 and 507 pictured in 1967 when just two years old. From the picture it will be noted that Marshall had improved its styling on the earlier Cambrette which is pictured above.*

THE VAM SERIES

As discussed earlier, the body builder Yeates had (controversially?) altered the SB chassis in order to provide a 44-seat, front-entrance body. This modification did not go down well with Vauxhall and considerable correspondence was generated over what became known as the FE44 project. Vauxhall said that such an arrangement would not work, but Yeates proved that it would. Part of the internal correspondence covering this period reveals that Vauxhall themselves were looking at providing a 44/48-seat front-entranced coach chassis, and Yeates had somehow stole their thunder.

In order to keep up with market trends, Bedford desperately needed a medium-sized front-entrance chassis, not so much to replace, but to supplement the SB chassis. The SB could obviously be adapted for front-entrance work, but only Yeates had really attempted such a design. It was therefore obvious that a production design was needed to satisfy market demand.

The VAL, at 36-feet (10.97m), whilst ideal for touring and a limited amount of fare-stage work, really did not provide the answer. While satisfying some customers (especially those doing motorway journeys), it proved to be too long a vehicle for most town and rural work. To alleviate this problem, Bedford unveiled their VAM (VA medium) chassis in the summer of 1965. This vehicle had a wheel base of 193-inches (4.9m). Like the VAL, it too had an 80-inch front overhang to allow the entrance door to be fitted ahead of the front axle. The seating capacity for this new chassis would be between 41- and 45-seats.

Discussions with both Duple and Plaxton prior to the launch of the VAM chassis ensured that the new offering would be satisfactory for bodying as a coach, service bus or dual purpose vehicle. The latter two variants were considered to be essential in the mid-1960s as operators were trying to find ways of combating the spiralling costs that were brought about by 'crew-manned' vehicles. The VAM was thus considered as an ideal one-man pay-as-you-enter bus!

Top Left: *This Bedford 1968 VAM (LFS 257F), has a 41-seat Duple body. The 6-ton 2-cwt bus is pictured outside Talanin House on the number 444 Eastern Scottish route to Kelso on 19th May 1969.*

Top Right: *Here a Bedford VAM carries a Strachans Paceway double door body. Pictured in 1967, it was designed for one man pay as you enter operation and became fleet number 824 with Hants & Dorset.*

Centre Right: *Walter Alexander & Co. Ltd of Falkirk built this bus on the Bedford VAM chassis for Highland Omnibuses, Inverness. It was operated on country routes with a rear compartment for freight served by a single near side door and double opening rear doors.*

Bottom Right: *This VAM has the MCW Metropolitan body, but it is probably the Metro-Cammell-Weymann Athena body after it was rebuilt. This picture dates from 1966 and the original documentation on the rear of the picture states that this has a 41/45-seat capacity. Yet examination of the records at Vauxhall proclaim that the body only had a capacity of between 32 and 41 seats.*

The VAM would have a choice of three engines, which were again front, vertically-mounted as in previous models. Designations were the VAM3, which had a Bedford 6-cylinder petrol engine with a 4.93 litre capacity; next came the VAM5 with a 5.42 litre 6-cylinder Bedford diesel engine; finally the third variant was the VAM14 which used the Leyland 0.400 6.17 litre diesel engine. However, in 1966 Bedford revealed a new diesel engine of 4.66 cubic inches at the Commercial Motor Show. This power unit developed 145bhp and meant that a Bedford-built option was now available throughout the company's truck and coach chassis range.

Even so, this unit was not made widely available to the PSV market until 1967 when it became the diesel option on the VAM. It was also the standard fitment for the VAL. More engine changes followed with the larger Bedford diesel engine replacing the Leyland power unit in the VAM 14, which then became the VAM70.

The VAM3 had an option of a 4 or 5-speed synchromesh gear-box, whilst the diesel-engined vehicles carried the 5-speed gear-box as standard. The VAM3 was also different from the diesel-engined versions as it used hydraulic-vacuum brakes as opposed to the hydraulic-air brakes. The complete range of VAM chassis were fitted with a hypoid-bevel rear axle. With the introduction of this model the VA range of Bedfords were now capable of catering for almost the entire seating capacity range for passenger transport up to the legally allowed 55-seat maximum. The complete VAM story is to feature in a later Trans-Pennine book, but the pictures on these two pages (and also in our companion book *Bedford Buses of the 1970s & '80s*) will give some idea of how versatile this chassis eventually became. Although not as popular as the SB, over 9,000 VAM chassis were built. It might best be remembered as the chassis on which Strachans, Willowbrook, Duple, Plaxton and Alexander all produced economical dual purpose or service bus bodies.

The VAL Series

Arguably one of Bedford's most famous achievements appeared in 1962, when together with more engine choices, a completely new three-axle chassis was unveiled. This, in fact, was not an entirely new concept, having been first attempted as early as 1922, when Bradford Corporation built a six-wheeled double-decker with steering fitted to both front axles. This design became known as the 'Chinese-Six' and although this particular idea was not to catch on for buses, it was to become well used on commercial trucks in later years. Indeed, the original Bradford bus- registered AK 9963 (Fleet No. 522), ran in the Corporation fleet for just five years. Another, better known vehicle was the 'Gnu' chassis, built by Leyland, and first shown at the 1937 Commercial Motor Show. This was designated TEP 1, and carried a 40-seater Alexander body with the front entrance situated some 5-feet ahead of it's front-most axle.

Aside from these designs, almost every other six-wheeled chassis was built to the standard design with a second single-wheeled axle at the rear. Typical of this layout were the AEC Renown, Leyland Titanic, and certain trolleybus applications built by Karrier. The three aforementioned vehicles being built in accordance with Ministry of Transport regulations then in force which dictated the use of a third axle for large capacity-carrying bodied vehicles.

Above: *A stunning good looker, and one of Bedford's 'Big Guns' is seen with this striking VAL photographed in January 1965. It carries the rare Harrington Legionnaire body, as this Hove-based firm built no more than 42 bodies for this type of chassis. Note the deep, wide windows and luxury seating within.*

Bedford's entrance into the six-wheeled chassis market was to once again prove highly successful with the new VAL being designed to cater for the then legally permitted 36-feet maximum vehicle length. Introduced in August 1962, and now also capable of carrying the legally allowed 55-seat maximum bodywork, the new vehicle was to prove however something of a challenge to the Bedford designers. Unlike all previous Bedford models, it is fair to claim that the VAL was to be the first true Bedford chassis to be prepared directly from the drawing board to the finished product specifically for bus and coach operations. True the OB and SB were bus orientated chassis, but they were derived from the O and S series truck chassis with certain SB chassis being re-developed in some cases by the body-builders themselves for specific types of PSV work. Another first for the VAL was the overhang of the chassis ahead of the front wheels. This now allowed the passenger door to be fitted at the very front of the vehicle, a design that was to be later emulated in the VAM chassis.

Top Right: *The VAL was not only used as a luxury coach chassis, but it also worked quite well as a dual purpose vehicle or service bus. This one was tailor-made for low bridges by the builder Strachans. This 36-ft long 52-seater bus on the Bedford VAL twin-steer passenger chassis was just one of ten bought by the North Western Road Car Company Ltd. They were ordered for use on North Western route 98 to pass under the Bridgwater canal at Dunham Woodhouses, but they got even further afield and I know they even operated on the express service from Manchester to Barnsley via Greenfield and Holmfirth. Their unladen height at the centre was only 9-foot 6-inches (2.89m) and 8-foot (2.43) at the cant rail above the window.*

Centre Right: *If the Strachans-VAL can be considered a good people mover, then the Marshall of Cambridge 'Airport Passenger Transport' body must be considered a great one. These bodies were built for a variety of airlines on the VAL14 chassis, including British European Airway (BEA), British Overseas Airways Corporation (BOAC), Trans-World Airlines (TWA) and Pan-American (PanAm) in the period 1963-1968. This one, LMG 159C (ex-BEA) dated from 1965, and later became British Airways fleet number C552. Other airlines used the VAL14 chassis as airport people-movers, including AerLingus who employed some wonderfully esoteric bodies*

Bottom Right: *Next we see the rare Metropolitan-Cammell-Weymann all-metal 49-seater Topaz body on the VAL14 chassis. It has a less-than-British look about it, and it is reported that MCW were looking for a coach body that could be exported in kit form to overseas customers, especially Australia and New Zealand. Looked at in this light, the Topaz could certainly fit the bill. Then there was the odd situation with re-bodying of one of the prototype VAL chassis, but on this point the records are unclear, yet someone out there must know the answer.*

As mentioned previously, the coachbuilders Yeates of Loughborough had achieved a true front-entrance Bedford when they modified the SB chassis to the FE44. However the VAL had now been purpose-built by Bedford for this requirement which gave all the coachbuilders a much neater layout with which to work.

One of the most unusual aspects of the design however, were the 16-inch wheels, now made famous by the earlier VAS model. Although now a familiar sight on Bedford vehicles they tended to look out of place, and somewhat ungainly on these new giant machines, but together with a soft suspension and another new innovation of fitting the shock-absorbers outside of the chassis frame, they gave passengers a much smoother ride.

Hydraulic power steering was fitted as standard. Also fitted was a re-circulating-ball steering box, which was of the worm and peg design. All steering connections were lubrication-free self-adjusting sealed joints. The turning circle for this model was 62-feet (18.9m) kerb to kerb, and 70-feet (21.3m) wall to wall. Wheels were 16-inch 3-piece, and 8.25x16 radial tyres were fitted all round.

SLOPE No1
14 1·4

825 CYR

Left: *Pictured on 5th May 1962, 825 CYR was a special VAL14 chassis constructed for experimental use (chassis number RHD62/2) and fitted with a Duple Vega Major body. It features seats from the Super Vega coach and is not provided with any form of luggage rack. The picture shows it undergoing rigorous testing on the 1 in 4 incline at the army test centre at Chobham, Surrey, 3 miles north-west of Woking. This coach apparently never entered PSV service.*

Top Right: *Duple Vega Major 825 CYR pictured on tilt test, in the window can be seen the cost of this vehicle at £3,625.00. Today that would work out at around £36,251, but it represented excellent value for money - little wonder they were so popular.*

Centre Right: *This VAL14-Duple Super Vega Major(213 SC) was used by Edinburgh Transport as a tourist exhibition unit. Chassis no. 1333 was one of six vehicles (213-218 SC) registered on the 1st May 1964. It was sold to Lewington's in May 1974 and was withdrawn in July 1974 after which it was used as a store shed. It is pictured here waiting to board a Townsend Ferry at Dover in January 1967.*

Bottom Right: *From left to right we see four members of the Baddeley Brothers fleet at Holmfirth bus station in 1963. Two Burlingham bodied Bedford SBs 2496 WY and 433 BWU are followed by Alpine Continental 474 EWW on a Leyland chassis and lastly 65 EWT. This 1963 VAL14 had chassis number 1113 and body number 1158/53. It was sold to Pollens of Dawley in October 1976 and scrapped in September 1980, but it was offered to my editor Alan Earnshaw for the sum of £350 in 1976 as a preservation project as it was his old school bus - sadly £350 (£1,500) was quite a lot of money in those days.* Alan Earnshaw

The original VAL14 power unit was the 6.17 litre Leyland 0.400 diesel engine, which was front-mounted and delivered 131bhp. A 14-inch single dry plate clutch was also fitted, with the American-designed gearbox providing five speeds, which had direct drive on 4th gear and overdrive on top gear. With synchromesh on all forward gears (with the exception of first), drive was continued through four open in-line propeller shafts with joints which were grease-packed for life. To reduce the amount of transmission-rumble reaching the body, all prop shaft chassis bearings were rubber mounted.

The rear axle was of the single-speed type, with three variants and a further option of a 2-speed axle was available on the model. Half shafts were fully-floating large diameter units, and the final drive was of the hypoid design, with an axle rating of 13,000lb.The chassis was fitted with channel section side members, which were swept downward and inwards at the front to give an easy-access low level entrance. Suspension was provided by six semi-elliptic springs with rubber-bushed spring eyes and shackles. Spring leaves were long and wide, with individual spring hangers that had positive first and second axle location in the event of a spring failure. Shock absorbers were six of the hydraulic double-acting telescopic type.

Top Left: *This is an extremely interesting series of pictures taken of the Vega Major body at Duple's Hendon works in 1965. Although this is clearly a Duple coach (note the raked rear windows) the interior has actually been taken from a Plaxton Panorama. The objective of the exercise was to test Plaxton's forced air conditioning system in the Duple interior. We have no detail on the identity of the coach, but does anyone recognise the headrest covers?*

Centre Left: *The next experiment was to try under-seat ventilation with blowers between the side panels and the edge of the seat. To create a lighter, brighter interior luggage racks were not fitted, and extra side lockers were provided instead.*

Bottom Left: *Finally, we show the conventional layout with aluminium framed luggage racks and the nylon mesh nets that were used to allow greater light penetration. This MkII model was demonstrated at the November 1965 Commercial Motor Show, but was only completed some four days before the event.*

Hydraulic air-pressure servo-assisted brakes operated on all six wheels via drums with an added safety feature of an over-riding mechanical operation from pedal to hydraulic cylinder should the servo fail. Independent hydraulic circuits were operated by a tandem-piston master cylinder, which was fitted as yet another safety feature. The handbrake operated on all four front wheels. The brake shoe linings were three inches (75mm) wide and made to allow the greatest friction with the least amount of fade possible.

Also fitted on the VAL was another safety feature (an auxiliary brake mounted on the prop-shaft towards the rear of the vehicle), which was fitted in the event that all the brakes failed. This was designed to stop the transmission or vehicle drive (as opposed to the road wheels direct) and was claimed to stop a fully laden vehicle from maximum speed in complete safety. However, after travelling through Aberdeen one Sunday morning in a Bedford VAS fitted with a similar arrangement, and the brakes failing as I approached a red traffic light, I feel one word was missing from this advertising 'spiel';..... **eventually!**

With a wheelbase of 231-inches (7.04m) and the new front entrance layout, the VAL also became an obvious choice for stage carriage work. The fact that when launched in 1962, a VAL chassis costing £1,775 (£19,312) was some £1,000 (£10,880) cheaper than any of it's rival underfloor engined bus/coach chassis was also of great significance.

By late 1967, the original VAL 14 was superseded by the VAL 70, which was now fitted with Bedford's own 466 cu inch 6-cylinder diesel engine of 7.63 litres capacity. This unit was fitted as a replacement for the original Leyland unit and was to be the standard fitting right through to the end of VAL production in 1972. The VAL design can also lay claim to two milestones achieved in the bus and coach story of 1965. Firstly the 50,000th passenger chassis was produced by Bedford; this being a VAL product bound for export to Australia. Also at about the same time, Duple completed their 25,000th body, this also being built on a VAL chassis.

On the coachbuilding side of things, there was no shortage of contenders willing to display their 'wares' on the new chassis, with (as ever) Duple being one of the early suppliers. The 52-seat Vega Major by Duple had similar characteristics as their Bella Vista design on the smaller VAS model, whilst they also catered for the fare-stage industry with their 55-seat service bus body. No-one can deny that the Vega Major was the undoubted success of the 1960s. It captured a market ready for change and it did so with style and panache, albeit with a body that did not last as long as its predecessors from the factory at Hendon.

The Vega Major-VAL combination came at precisely the right time for the small independent operators. It was inexpensive, it was attractive, it had superb capacity, and what was more the new motorways, dual carriageways and clearways were opening fast routes to the major cities, towns and seaside resorts. Furthermore the Conservative government had appointed Dr. Richard Beeching (an accountant from the ICI) to wield his ferocious axe on Britain's railway network. With seaside branch lines being decimated overnight, and no reprieve coming from the newly elected Labour government, countless thousands of seaside-bound day trippers and holiday-makers were left without the means of 'getting away from it all'.

When one considers that even little seaside stations like Withernsea in Yorkshire (closed October 1964) had upwards of 25 excursion trains a day in the height of summer, from places like Bradford, Leeds, Hull and Sheffield, it is little wonder that a substantial number of motor coaches were needed to replace them. Consider the following statistics:

On August Bank Holiday Monday 1964 no less than 21,061 passengers had arrived at this basic resort - just think how many might have arrived by rail at Blackpool, Southport, Clacton or Brighton. Even if the stations at these major resorts were still open, many 'excursion' stations like those at Blackpool and Scarborough were closed due to a serious loss of traffic. After all if the station in your home village or town had closed down, then there was little point in travelling by service bus to the nearest railhead to catch an excursion or holiday train from there - you might as well go by motor coach. It was a coach operator's charter, and one the enterprising firm of the 1960s would not ignore.

Top Right: *Another view of the 1965 Motor Show showing the new Vega Major MkII by Duple featuring repositioned twin headlamps, re-styled front and rear end. The body price for this vehicle was £3,995 (£51,935) and the exhibited price was £4,505 (£58,565). The vehicle shown here was destined for Smiths of Reading.*

Centre Right: *Here is the Duple 53-seater metal-framed VAL 14 service bus, which had an unladen weight of 5-ton 17-cwt. As this Duple demonstrator shows, the combination looked very basic indeed.*

Bottom Right: *In August 1966 the new FS64 body range was announced by Duple to replace the Vista/Vega series. This was better known as the Viceroy range and here, pictured on a VAL 14 chassis, is the 1967/8 Viceroy 35 body (Grey-Green Coaches SYX 577F), which by now has the optional one-piece screen.*

As the new Vega Major-VAL combination was such good value, and could carry an almost equivalent passenger capacity to the standard British Railways MkI passenger coach, investment in one of these vehicles was bound to pay dividends. One operator, Geoffrey Wainwright of Abbeyways Coaches (Halifax) once told us that in those days a coach would pay for itself inside a year. Indeed, at the time he took delivery of one vehicle or batch of vehicles, he would be ordering its replacements for twelve months hence. In fact, there was also a big demand for good quality second-hand vehicles, so a one-year-old coach could often be sold at a profit on its purchase price. So, when you look at the available records and see how often a VAL changed hands in its early life, you would be staggered to note that many had moved on to new owners within 24-months of purchase. Yet, further examination will show that the majority of those owners selling the Bedford VAL-Duple Vega Major combination, were replacing it with exactly the same model.

This trend continued through the 1960s, but Duple rather missed out on what would become a market dominated by the Plaxton Panorama because it stayed with the Vega Major a might too long.

The trend of the 1960s had gone towards light, airy coaches with big windows and good ventilation. Plaxton scored in all these areas with their new Panorama because it had large windows and superb forced air ventilation ducts mounted in passenger-controlled vents above each seat - and these were great devices for stopping little Bobby from feeling sick after eating too much candyfloss on the beach at Blackpool.

Now, as some of the accompanying pictures clearly show, Duple looked very closely at the Plaxton interior, but they never got their offering quite right and they retained smaller windows with sliding vents to satisfy these needs. At one stage, after the Burlingham acquisition, it was decided that the way ahead was to adapt the Alpine Continental bodywork (see picture on page 45) and make this fit the VAL chassis. As it was, Duple decided that the VAL chassis was too light for this European-influenced body, and it remained primarily on AEC and Leyland chassis, but there are suggestions in the Bedford record that one greatly modified Alpine Continental body was fitted to a VAL chassis for test. More information on this would be appreciated.

Top Left: *After the 1962 Motor Show the VAL 14 prototype chassis number RHD62/1 had its Weymann body removed and given a Plaxton experimental body. This body (No.2225) was called the Plaxton VAL and featured a modified version of the Embassy. It had been fitted to prototype chassis LHD62/3 and this picture is said to be taken of it early in 1963 by Plaxton's photographer, but it has a distinct look of the coach that was registered 477 CTM.*

Top Right: *Experimental chassis RHD62/1 then became 472 DYK and was later modified for use as a racing car transporter for Jack Brabham. The front half retained the passenger carrying space, but the rear part was converted to form a transporter body for Formula 1 cars that gained access to the load space via a lift-up tailgate.*

Centre Right: *Again with 'Embassy-styling' 375 RVO was an early Plaxton Panorama C49F (body number 632551) on VAL14 chassis number 1081. It was supplied in April 1963 to William Moxons of Oldcotes, and is shown here at Lady Bower Reservoir, Derbyshire.*

Bottom Right: *The more common Plaxton-VAL 14 combination was one of the hardest pictures to find, as all those in the Vauxhall record were missing. Here we see EUG 916D, one of a batch of MkI Plaxton Panorama coaches supplied new to Wallace Arnold of Leeds. It later went to Top Line of Ravensthorpe near Dewsbury.* Martin Perry

Even though the Alpine Continental was not developed the Vega Major remained a popular coach and it even found fame as a Dinky Toy model. Its successor was the Duple Viceroy, which had an angular and dated feel about it at a time when Plaxton were making sweeping improvements to the early Panorama. Indeed, it was not until the new Dominant began to appear on the Bedford chassis of the 1970s, that Duple would regain the edge it had lost to the Panorama in the mid-1960s. Conversely the Plaxton offering on the VAL chassis had started off looking like an ugly extension of a relatively dated (conventional???) design and it did little to inspire anyone to buy the Scarborough-built product.

Yet, when the Panorama came out, it looked as though it was built for the chassis, and it found favour with many operators. This included several long-haul operators who were running the VAL-Panorama combination on some substantial runs. We know of at least two who did European tours down to the South of France in the mid-1960s, using Bedfords where they had previously used AEC chassis.

As the 1960s continued, so did improvements on the Panorama, and towards the end of the decade these culminated with the Panorama Elite, which embodied a number of subtle changes that operators had been asking for. So, as our era comes to an end, we see that both Plaxton and Duple had much to offer the coach-operating fraternity, but we should not forget that their were other builders who also found the new Bedford VAL an ideal platform on which to build for the ever-expanding holiday, day tour, private hire and motorway service markets.

Top Left: *Carrying the Panorama Elite body, MND 214G (chassis number 9T466196) was one of two VAL70s bought by Manchester City Transport in May 1969. It is seen here on the SELNEC (South East Lancashire North East Cheshire) Hale Barns Express outside Manchester's Opera House. The coach was sold to Sidat & Afzal of Blackburn in May 1978 but it was withdrawn within the month. Sister vehicle MND 213G was sold to Hughes of Rhyl in September 1978, but both had seen considerable service (and wear) with the PTE.*

Centre and Bottom Left: *Next we have two views of HNK 149G (chassis number 7T459398) fitted with Plaxton Panorama Elite C53F bodywork (No.692406) which was new to Sonners of Chatham, Kent in March 1969. The coach was sold to Newland Crow of Kent in May 1974 but was damaged by fire in January 1982. The two views here, show it when brand new and still carrying Plaxton posters and Arlington's trade plates numbered 395 NK.*

One rare design on the VAL chassis, and indeed a relative newcomer to the Bedford fold, was Metropolitan-Cammell-Weyman (MCW), with their Topaz body. This, together with Duple's service bus was of all-metal construction, as opposed to most other designs, which were of composite (metal frame with wooden inserts) build. An original advertising brochure for the Topaz described it as an 'attractive 49-seat body offering spacious and comfortable passenger accommodation together with an exceptional degree of economy and long life. All-metal weight saving construction gives immediate savings in performance and economy'. Yeates of Loughborough also bodied the VAL with their Fiesta and Europa models, but the dual-entry Europa versions produced for the major operator Barton (with large In/Out lettering by the doors) was hardly the most attractive finish; especially when compared to the Yeates-bodied VALs supplied to operator like Rickards or Gibsons.

A much more pleasing design was the Legionnaire by Harrington of Hove, who built just 42 examples to their design. Two members of this batch of coaches (CNW 154-5C) were new to Heaps of Leeds, and of these CNW 155C is now owned by Trans-Pennine Publishing, the producers of this book. Harrington would go to any lengths to secure an order for this model, and as an example the two Heaps coaches were fitted with leopard skin pattern moquette to match their 'leaping leopard' motif on the coach sides. It is also a coach on which I am destined to spend many an hour in an order to get it back to full operational status. Some of the Legionnaire coaches were also supplied to Barton. Possibly the most famous VAL coach is the Harrington Legionnaire ALR 453B (ex-Batten Coaches), which was used to transport the three mini cars in the Michael Caine-Noel Coward film *The Italian Job*.

Other builders included Marshall, Willowbrook and Strachans, the latter supplying a batch of dome-roof VALs to North Western Road Car Co. to combat a low bridge problem. The sheer size of the VAL also made it popular with various airports for passenger transfer duties, it is also the 'cult' coach of the 1960s and as such it is also the subject of a future book in the **Nostalgia Road Premier Series**.

Mind you, we should not forget that the VAL was also something of a success in the export market as well. Two of the original prototypes were made as left-hand drive versions, although one of these was later converted back to rhd. This coach was in some way connected with the odd decision to swap the Weyman body, but the reasons for this change have been lost in the mists of time and are missing from the Vauxhall records. But, if you know the answer......??? Some of the overseas body styles were odd to say the least, and we have one picture of what can only be a shed-cum-greenhouse on VAL wheels. This oddity was operated by a firm called Susheila and appears to have had a 60- or 62-seat capacity. Other than the fact that the picture arrived at Dunstable works on 31st May 1965, we have no other information about it.

Down-under, in both Australia and New Zealand, the VALs were widely appreciated, and many are still working there today. Yet the VAL has not entirely disappeared from the British scene either, and there are one or two (mostly VAL 70s) still at work today. There are others that still hold a soft spot for their owners, and at the time of writing I can tell of one Blackpool operator who still has a VAL 70-Viceroy combination parked at the back of his garage. 'It still has its original paintwork and is as good as new' he told me proudly at a recent coach rally.

It was much the same with John Hood of Wold Newton who sold his VAL14-Legionnaire to Trans-Pennine last November after it stood for 20 years in the back of its garage following damage to the front nearside windscreen. John said, 'I just couldn't think of scrapping it somehow, it was too good a coach for that. It made me a lot of money after I bought it, and I hoped that one day someone would come along and put it right again.' Well that is just what I am hoping to do in the months ahead, and you could say that I've now become a convert. So, I hope that like me, you too will have become a convert to the Bedford Marque after reading all of this. And if any one is so influenced as to actually want to lend some support (practical, moral or financial) towards the restoration of the SB, the VAS and the VAL that we are now undertaking, I'd be delighted to hear from you care of the publishers!

Top Right: *Seen outside the General Motor dealers in Lundstein is one of the VALs exported to Denmark. Previous publications have reported that only one VAL (the Soro C48F-bodied AS 99.252) was supplied to Viking Bus, part of the Danish Continental Bus Lines. Yet from this photograph it is obvious that at least one more VAL went to this fleet as here we see KA 79.173. The body maker is not recorded.*

Centre Right: *It has also been written that only two VALs were ever sent to New Zealand but again we know this to be incorrect. Here we see a VAL14 C49F supplied by General Motors, New Zealand, to Midland Coaches and registered P3.384.*

Bottom Right: *This VAL14 for Days Motors of Christchurch, was supplied by the New Zealand Farmers' Co-operative Association and was the third to be built on a VAL chassis for that company alone. Designed to give maximum comfort to tourists the new bus was notable for the high standard of luxury provided for its 36 passengers.*

ACKNOWLEDGMENTS

This book would not have been possible without the very kind assistance of a large number of people, with some of whom I have had only a passing contact: Although some only played a small or unknowing part, their help has been vital in completing the book. Others had no actual part in this story, but they still helped inspire me in the preservation movement. So in conclusion I must thank:-

Tony Anstruther
Robert Berry
Tony & Ashley Blackman
Blackpool Library Service
Peter Blincow
British Airways
Tony Burnip
Terry Calvert
Jeff Colledge
Ray Cooper
Dave Dexter
Brian Duncan
Alan & Larraine Earnshaw
Barry Harvey
John Hood

Gordon & Robert Jamieson
Pat Isbister
Marc Knott
Philip Lamb
Peter and Andrew Leask
Martin Perry
John Purves
Matthew & Bryony Richardson
Dennis Sherer
Louise Tarn
David Townend
Vauxhall Motors
Walsall Library Service
Richard Walton, and
Bob Wingrove

and above all I must say a sincere thank you to my wife **Jackie,** and also my daughters Michaela, Laura and Georgia for putting up with all my absences during the research and writing of this book. I wonder if they will be so forgiving when I tell them that I am involved in writing the next book in the series - *Bedford Buses of the 1960s & '70s*.

I hope that you will join Jeff Colledge and I, as we conclude the Bedford bus story.